a New Gateway for Venice

International Venice Studio

WORKSHOP
UNSW Built Environment Sydney

Edited by Paola Favaro, Anna-Paola Pola and Katrina Simon
Graphic coordination by Anna-Paola Pola

Index

Introduction
page 4 - 5

Venice in the current
metropolitan system
by Enrico Fontanari,
Università IUAV di Venezia
page 6 - 13

Venice is a modern city
by Paola Favaro,
UNSW Built Environment
page 14 - 23

On Immersion As
An Architectural Strategy
by Katrina Simon,
UNSW Built Environment
page 24 - 29

Permanence and Change
in the Historic City
by Anna-Paola Pola,
Università IUAV di Venezia
page 30 - 39

Venice in transformation
CONVERSATION with
Alberto Cecchetto
page 40 - 43

Design and history
CONVERSATION
with Alberto Ferlenga
page 44 - 47

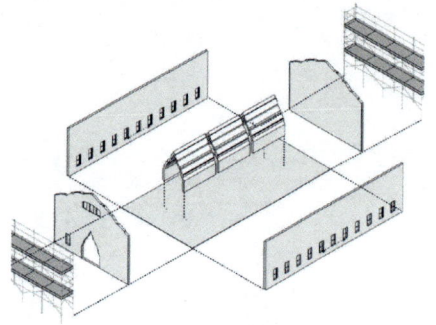

Urban Survey and Design
by Paola Favaro
page 48 - 53

Nexus 1
Catriona Bisset, Jackie Lee, Vanessa Wood, Shen Jia, Omer Mosman, Andrea Tommasin
page 54 - 61

central courtyard

Reclaiming Venice 2
Aurelie Nguyen, Mingmin Liu, Nadia Hendryani, Julia Lau, Simone Rego, Marco de Stavola, Micol Galeotti
page 62 - 69

calles/entry points

Impermanence 3
Amber Gallen, Enrica Pavan, Francesco Orteschi, John Ellice-Flint, Jun Loh
page 70 - 77

pushing and pulling the building form based on surrounding program

Coalescence 4
Meidan Yin, Jonathan Yip, Lisa Cohen, Parise Chyssargis, Lubna Matar
page 78 - 85

The Treasure of Venice 5
Allison Sainty, Ashleigh Bennett, Marco Carraro, Niloofar Meshgini, Tommaso Gomiero, Yvonne Chan
page 86 - 93

Giardini of the West 6
Annie Tran, Dean Kim, Fabio Matteazzi, Jessica Li, Maria Imbrigliati, Rawail Khan
page 94 - 101

Introduction

In November 2014, the International Venice Studio (IVS) created for the third time the opportunity for staff and students from the Master of Architecture at the University IUAV of Venice (Italy) and in the disciplines of Architecture, Landscape Architecture and Interior Architecture from the University of New South Wales (UNSW), Sydney (Australia) to work together as a joint urban and architectural design studio.

A selected number of approximately 26 students from the three UNSW disciplines of architecture, landscape and interior, a group of 12 Italian students from the host University IUAV of Venice (IUAV) and 3 visiting students at the IUAV coming from the Future University of Khartoum (Sudan), were engaged in a critical discourse on contemporary problems of the built environment grounded in the culture of Venice. The site and nature of the project was related to the un-renovated "Gas Area" in the neighbourhood of Santa Marta, located in the west part of the Historic Centre of Venice.

In the two weeks of intense-block mode of seminars and traditional design studio, students were also challenged by two days of preliminary visit to the Biennale of Architecture in Giardini and Arsenale (curator that year was Rem Koolhaas), the visit to the contemporary urban projects realized at the end of last century in Giudecca Island and other specific site visits, independently taken by the students, prior or during the studio activity.

The IVS involved the production of a series of two and three-dimensional drawings of site and precedent analysis and the design and/or re-design of a selected site(s) into a series of meaningful spatial ambiances, connected through a structural logic of relationships: physically, visually and conceptually.
By investigating Venice's historical urban system and urban typologies as well as specific historical and current precedents, students questioned aspects of urban landscape, architectural forms and interior spaces, exploring the opportunity to redevelop

1. The first editions of the IVS were realized in 2010, "Reshaping Venice", working on the urban redevelopment area in the island of Santa Elena, in the east part of the historic city, and in 2013, "Glamour Marghera", working on the proposal of a new Cruise Terminal and an urban renewal project to be realized in the brownfield of Marghera, on the edge of the Lagoon facing Venice from west.

the Gas Area from the outside to the inside (the site and the design challenges of the IVS are described in the first chapter). Aspects of space/form, movement and activity were tested against students' appreciation of the physical setting and environment of the urban context where the case studio is located and the social concerns of the historical city. Three distinct but complementary components from the three disciplines of architecture, landscape (urban landscape, but also the landscape of the Lagoon were deeply analysed) and interior design were eventually finalised as part of the new urban configuration.

By the end of the two intense weeks, the collaboration between the two schools was evident in the students' final presentation, where it was tangible how the students were able to:
- discern that their integrated design of spaces and volumes related to the existing geographical and historical context, which was based on a through understanding of selected architecture, urban and natural landscape and interior precedents, and influenced by ideas from all the three disciplines;
- work creatively within and across disciplines, with each student learning from the insights of the other students;
- utilize research and analysis coming from diverse sources in an 'imaginative', 'creative' and 'operative' manner, interpreting these through two and three dimensional graphic representation;
- clearly articulate and clearly define a strategic urban vision and a rigorous design position from its conceptual stage to a developed design proposal;
- first envision and then create a series of interior and urban spaces, which responded to a particular event, activity and socio-cultural environment in the project site of the "Gas Area".

Photo of the project area, the ex-ItalGas, in Venice.

Venice in the current metropolitan system

Enrico Fontanari

Venice is a city with a long glorious history, a difficult present and an uncertain future.

The historic town is an incredible concentration of historic paintings, frescos and sculptures, historic buildings and monuments, all inserted in a unique landscape. The great heritage value of the city attracts around 30 million tourists every year and represents a great economic resource, but at the same time, it is the greatest threat for the city life.
The main danger is represented by the actual trend of the urban economy which is progressively transforming itself into a form of "mono-sectorial" economy, i.e. creating an urban economy based only on tourist activities. Many studies on the tourist economy have shown that if this economic sector is the only economic activity in one place (like, for example, in the ocean islands and archipelagos dedicated only to the "sun and beach" tourism), it will slowly destroy the resources which originally generated those kind of activities and riches.
Something similar could happen to Venice, slowly transforming the historic town into a new Disneyland. The big issue related with the actual government of the possible urban transformations, is how to avoid loosing the characteristics of a living city with mixed uses. Venice is actually slowly transforming itself into an inhabited theme park.
To avoid this danger, the urban policies, which the local authorities implemented in the town have always tried to maintain and protect the residential use and to promote the presence of other economic activities, like the educational use (the entire historic city of Venice can be a perfect campus) and the enterprises related to the cultural and creative economy. Cultural tourism is not a danger to the town. The main problems are related to the massive presence of daily visitors (in 2014 we had about

30 millions visitors, staying in towns on average 6 hours from Venice). This kind of pressure is changing the small daily commerce by abandoning the commercial offer to the residents offering instead selling points of very low quality products for quick tourists (selling hamburgers and hot dogs, fake masks and glass products made in other countries, t-shirts and other objects for one euro, etc.). To stop this trend it is important to support the residential use by ensuring the presence of different city users, like the students, the employers of the private offices and of the public administration (the city and regional governments are still located in the historic city), artists, curators and other representatives of the creative world and of the cultural environment (museums, galleries, etc.).

With reference to this issue, one important way, from an urban planning point of view, is to strengthen the relationship of the historic center with the urban areas of the main land. From a general point of view, the aim is to build a vision for the city of Venice as the Historic Center of a wider metropolitan area that goes from Mestre-Marghera to the cities of Padova and Treviso, a metropolitan area called with an acronym "Patreve".

This means to go beyond the condition of "island" of the old town settled in the lagoon reinforcing instead its links with the key area of the lagoon edge, acting on the important issue of the accessibility to the town and the transport links with the

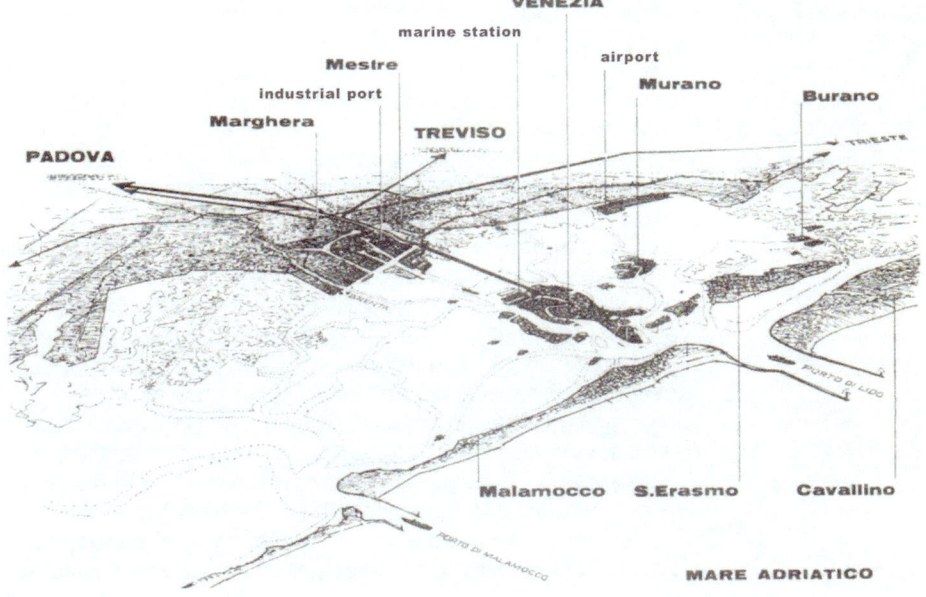

Relationship of the historic centre and its metropolitan urban settlement

main land. The west part of the old town of Venice is therefore a key area, it is the place that can help solving this problem in a positive way.

By reinforcing the accessibility and the mobility link of Venice with the mainland, it will also strengthen the role of Venice in the urban system of the Veneto Region. Venice represents the international image of the entire Region, but particularly it can be considered as the international "face" of the big metropolitan area "Patreve", which will became the most important urban settlement of the North-East part of Italy.

The North-East is an Italian Region characterized by the so called "urban dispersion", a wide urbanized region with a large diffusion of small settlements, spread throughout the plain region between Milan and Venice.

It is considered a polycentric region, but in reality there are mostly small urban centers, 45 centers have less then 50.000 inhabitants, two have between 50.000 and 100.000 inhabitants on average, and only three bigger towns have between 200.000 and 300.000 inhabitants.

What is really needed in the North-East is to build the "sense" of the city abandoning the actual condition of conflictive coexistence of small centers, each one fighting against the other, and to realize a new town system transforming the polycentrism into one real city. Modern metropolitan areas are sites where contemporary services and financial enterprises, creative industries and other innovative activities are concentrated and not dispersed in several small localities. Thus, the contemporary city is one strong and united productive machine.

This brings for this area of the Veneto Region, and particularly for the areas around the town of Venice, the necessity to build a metropolitan ecosystem, which could lead to the realization of an urban settlement that is in a position to be competitive with other urban areas in Europe and to be able to attract investments, knowledge, skillful social immigration from other areas. The realization of a metropolitan ecosystem could facilitate the localization of new productive activities, linked to the creative and cultural economy and in general to the new society of knowledge. In this field the historic city of Venice, with its renowned international appeal, can play an important role.

The urbanized area including the three towns of Padova, Treviso and Venice (the "Patreve) has already reached the characteristics of a polycentric metropolitan area. In terms of residential areas, urban services and equipment, universities, hospitals, etc., this vast area is well equipped. And in the last years also the mobility system has grown in this area, based on

A night shot of the North-East Region

the public transport by rail, bus and tram. But indeed in the field of mobility there is still much to do and this is the main scenario that the Venice Gateway workshop has faced.

A new Venice Gateway

The urban issue faced by this intensive design workshop is the possibility of designing a new Gateway to Venice in the western part of the historic city. Here there is a large abandoned area of the previous public gas company "Veneziana Gas".
This area is accessible by car as it is the entrance to the old commercial harbour and is directly invested by the project of the extension of a new line of tram. The new tram will link the Historic city directly with the mainland city of Mestre and Marghera, with the airport and with the future high speed train station in Mestre. The area is also facing a large canal, with an easy access from the lagoon system and already has a public service waterbus stop.
In the new 2014 Master Plan for the town of Venice, the area is presented as an area for urban redevelopment, with the possibility to realize new residential use, open spaces and facilities, a new accessibility to the old town, parking, etc..
The residential use is considered a main goal of the master plan, as this is the main problem that the city is currently facing to resist the ongoing process of gentrification. The historic center has lost many inhabitants in the last 20 years. In the 1980s there were more then 90.000 residents in the historic city in comparison with the recent situation of an average of 60.000 residents.

The accessibility system:
yellow / Mestre highway bypass
black / main roads
blue / regional railway
red / tram
light blue / navigation lines

The previous 1998 Master Plan had started a first process of realization of new residential neighborhoods in the island of la Giudecca, on the site of abandoned industrial activities in the south front of the island. The 2014 recent master plan proposes to add to that intervention the realization of new dwellings in empty areas located in the periphery of the town, of which nearly 800 have already been built. The western part of Venice, our workshop site, the abandoned "Gas Area", is one of the most interesting sites which could shortly undergo this process.
The new residential use intends to propose a mixed housing system. This system includes the realization of public housing at a very low cost (including dwellings for students), dwellings to be sold at a controlled price and part to be sold on the free market by the private investors, called to realize the intervention in form of a "project financing".
The residential area has to be integrated with areas for public services, sport facilities, green areas and other open spaces,

The Gas Area in Venice

etc.. A new tram is supposed to pass by the canal, as part of the new tram lines already under construction to link Mestre to Venice (about 6,5 km), to be integrated with the existing line of 12,5 km already built within the settlements of Mestre, Favaro and Marghera.
The empty Gas Area is adjacent to an existing residential area (the area of Santa Marta) realized at the beginning of the XX° century, which is now isolated and partly segregated. Something has changed with the location which is the most important teaching campus of the IUAV University (Faculties of Architecture, Industrial and Fashion Design, Visual Art and Theatre), but the new project proposed for this site by the 2014 master plan, with the implementation of the residential use and the introduction of public services and new open areas, could for sure change completely the appeal of this urban zone reinforcing its urban identity.
By integrating this residential intervention with the realization of buildings for cultural use, the entire area of West Venice, now mainly a periphery with large abandoned industrial sites, could change its character and could become an integrated urban site representing the new urban west frontier of the historic city. The new cultural activities in synergy with the main existing activities like the Biennale and with the presence of the university will be realized also with the adaptation of many old harbour buildings. By recognizing the potential of this area with new interventions and with the adaptation of existing empty or underutilized spaces the students' proposals will ultimately represent a new scenario for this area.

A New Gateway for Venice is therefore an opportunity to redesign the western part of Venice by:
- improving the accessibility from the mainland to the historic city, creating a new entrance with public transport (tram), which will open the south part of the city for the daily commuting with the mainland, representing a real alternative to the actual bus terminal of Piazzale Roma and facilitating in particular the access to the universities located in the area of Santa Marta;
- reinforcing the residential character of the historic center, improving at the same time the urban quality of the entire area of Santa Marta, creating a greater demand of services which can justify the location of more public services, green open spaces, commercial uses, local markets, etc., for the local neighbourhood;
- improving the presence of the students in the town as city users, building new dorms in this area, and in the same time

reinforcing the west part of the town as great campus;
- balancing the cultural offer of Venice, which is now mostly concentrated in the east part of the town (in the neighbourhoods of Castello and San Marco) and in the area of La Salute;
- building, consequently, in that area contemporary architecture of high quality for this new cultural use, with new constructions also in the area of the old harbour, which all together will represent a new symbolic "entrance door" for the city, a glamourous modern urban façade;
- facilitating the recovery of many abandoned old industrial buildings, which are now in danger and risk to be demolished.

Urban design in Venice

The workshop has also represented the opportunity to experiment a contemporary new architecture and urban design in the historic city.
As well described in the P. Favaro's essay, Venice has always had a difficulty in accepting the insertion of modern architecture in its historic urban fabric. In the past the city refused the projects of important representatives of the modern move-

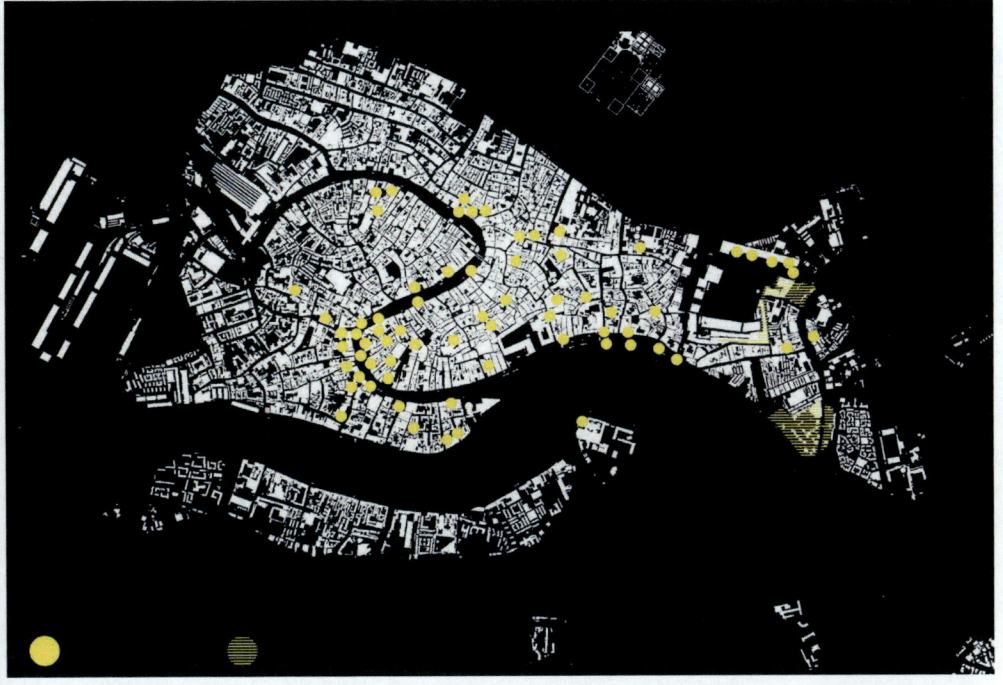

Actual location of the main cultural spaces

ment (like F.L. Wright, Le Corbusier, L. Kahn) and accepted some only if located in the periphery and with limited punctual interventions (G. De Carlo, G. Valle). Particularly in the second half of the last century, the urban management of the town was concentrated in the promotion of restoration and urban rehabilitation interventions, which has been very important and useful (see the essay of A.P. Pola), but limited the construction of good contemporary architecture. The compulsory reference to the original urban typologies and urban morphology, very important if applied to the urban restoration, became a limitation for the realization of new interventions and new buildings. By the end of the last century, with the new 1998 Master Plan, things changed and the interventions in the south part of the island of la Giudecca represent the creation of a new trend in the town. Recently, new experimental architectural languages have been accepted in the lagoon landscape to include among others the residential building of C. Zucchi, the rehabilitation and new intervention in historic buildings T. Ando in Punta della Dogana at La Salute and R. Piano in the Magazzini del Sale at the Zattere.

This new trend creates a condition of more "design freedom" thanks to the contribution of the students, who can introduce new ways of looking at the town, with a new interpretation of the urban landscape and the consequent proposals of insertion of contemporary architecture.

In Venice the urban design proposals have to face many constraints:
- the relationship with a clear typological structure of the residential buildings, which can easily be recognized in the poor and also the rich palaces;
- the general use in the town of traditional materials, like wood, bricks and white stones in the buildings and the grey stones for the road pavement;
- the presence of a complex urban morphology, characterized by the narrow streets, the different open spaces, the passages below the houses, the path along the canals and the bridges of different forms and dimensions;
- the difficulty of the insertion of new buildings in a strong and clearly defined urban landscape, with vertical signs, horizontal lines and a compact urban mass;
- the relationship with the canals and in general with the particular landscape of the lagoon and of an urban form settled on a system of islands.

At the same time, this complex urban and landscape condition represents an opportunity to develop innovative design proposals both in the architectural and urban field. By introducing new languages in the facades, different but compatible materials, unexpected design of the open and of the green spaces opened to the various city users and integrated with a changed interior design.
That was the main challenge that the students faced during the international workshop, producing at the end innovative, ambitious and provocative solutions, which represented a very good final output.

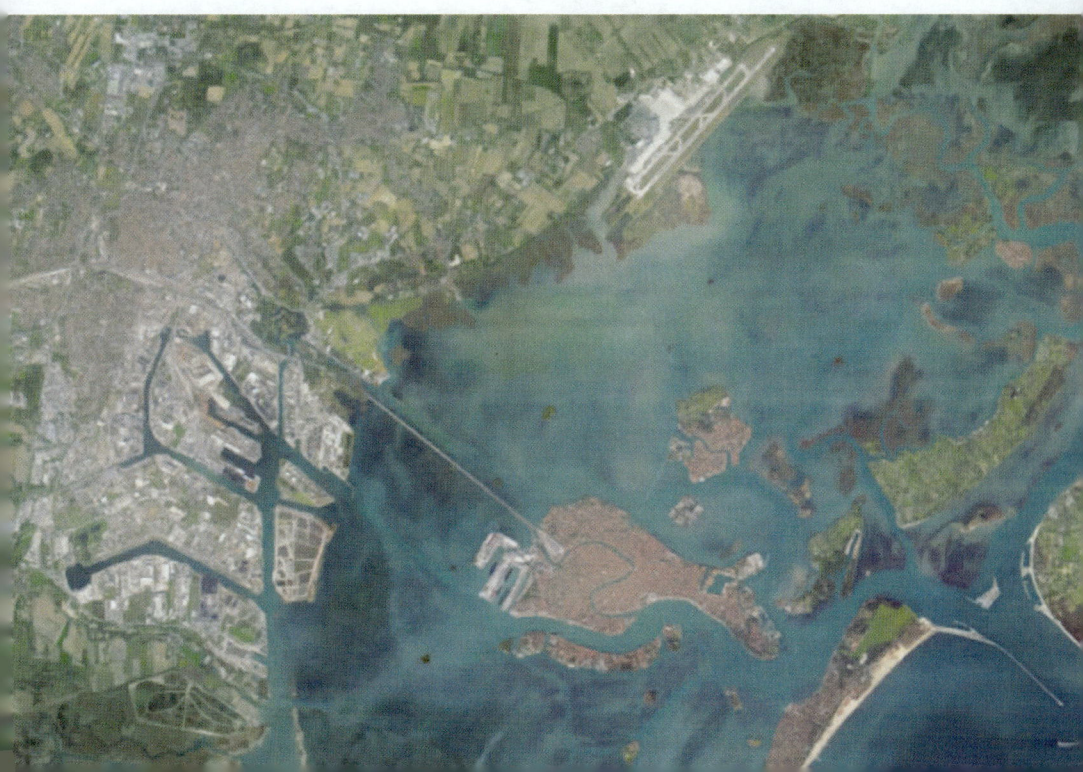

Venice and Mestre

Venice as a modern city

Paola Favaro

Le Corbusier, Venice CIAM School 1952

"Venice is my model for every city of the future"
So wrote Swiss architect and urban designer, Le Corbusier, in his book of 1935, *La Ville Radieuse: elements d'une doctrine d'urbanism pour l'equipement de la civilization machinist.*

In the years that followed, Le Corbusier forged a strong involvement with the city of Venice. As an educator he participated in the 1952 Venice CIAM (Congrès Internationaux d'Architecture Moderne) School. As a designer he contributed to the planning in 1964 of the unrealized project for the Venice Hospital, which was to be built in the San Giobbe neighborhood in the Cannaregio area.
In both instances he praised Venice as a model worthy of emulation for every future city. Le Corbusier had particular regard for the city's habitat which was based on the original city infrastructure (self-contained insulae – island) or neighborhoods. Likewise, he paid homage to the significance of the wide-open space of the campo (square) as the organizing system of movement and urban activity. Through this engagement, Lo Stato di Mar (State of Sea) and Lo Stato di Terra (State of Land) came to represent the centuries-old dialectic between the layers of this city in its continuity as both

an urban system and an architecture system. It is no coincidence that Le Corbusier's project for the Venice Hospital shifted the 1960s architecture attention to 'organization' and ordering systems as historical recognizable urban configurations from 'imagery' and shape-making. This latter notion was explored by Manfredo Tafuri (Tafuri 1989) and Colin Rowe (Rowe 2002) in their reading of Venice as a Renaissance city. (Mumford 2001).

A comprehensive analysis of Le Corbusier's Venice Hospital is beyond the scope of this chapter, yet by adopting his approach to analysis and design we can better understand the historical framework of Venice. The latter stands out as a design tool – something that continues to influence the current design process of the Venice Studio and which has also informed contemporary Venetian architecture in the last twenty years, as documented by Renata Codello in her recent publication (Codello 2014).

Ordering System

Eighty years after Le Corbusier made his statement, can we still regard Venice as a model for the city of the future? The answer to these questions lies in a discussion of the city as an example of urban architecture. The architect and urban designer, Franco Mancuso, argues in Venezia e' una citta' that architecture and the city are one and the same thing: the urbanistica becomes architettura, and conversely architettura becomes urbanistica.

In Venice the land has never existed a priori. This is at odds with every other city in Italy, and possibly throughout the world, where growth is determined by the subdivisions of the land, the organization of the infrastructure and eventually the construction of the buildings. The urban elements of the city of Venice with their unique names of campo, inter alia, campiello, calle, ruga, fondamenta, salizzada, were constructed concurrently with the architecture of the buildings. Thus, to realize a building on the canal meant consolidating both the banks and also the relation of the building to the open space of the calle and campo. In Venice the urban design, the urbanistica, the overall form of the city is more important than the individual buildings. (Mancuso, 2009)

Whether the vantage point is the Campanile di San Marco, or the Campanile di San Giorgio Maggiore (from where Jacopo de' Barbari most likely drew the Pianta Prospettica di Venezia del 1500), the dense urban fabric of the city is established by the relation of the buildings to the canals. Consider this as a continuous homogeneous mat punctuated by the towers and cupolas of the churches and public buildings. Indeed, Venice appears compact, a city that built to its edges with nowhere to grow; a whole, defined entity, or what the architecture historian Manfredo Tafuri called an *organic whole*, a built environment consolidated over the centuries. Closer study and observation reveal a different reading of Venice, which suddenly transforms the organic whole into a dynamic city where renovations, adaptations and new constructions continue to this day.

Le Corbusier's question can also be answered by acknowledging that Venice is its architecture, and the architecture is the city. Perhaps the only way to sustain his 1935 argument is to recognize that as an example of urban architecture Venice highlights the city's historic relationship with water and the land. For Le Corbusier the system of the insula and their evolution into a cluster, formed a continuous fabric of differentiated urban spaces centered in the wide-open place of the campo. The campi as the organizing system of the urban activities were far more important for Le Corbusier than the architecture of the surrounding residential buildings, or of the dominant presence of religious and representative buildings often giving the name to the campo. Le Corbusier added weight to his view in his 1952 address to the Venice CIAM School, pointing out how the city is "made of elements so clear that we see here surge and manifest all the problems of architecture and urbanism". (Valle 1952)

Urban Architecture

The term urban architecture aptly describes the relation between urban system and architecture system and was re-valuated and brought to a new appreciation by the 1950s CIAM (Congrès Internationaux d'Architecture Moderne) congresses. From its much-celebrated beginning in 1928 at La Sarraz, Switzerland, to its official ending in 1959 at Otterlo, Netherlands, CIAM represented a progressive discourse in architecture and urbanism, influencing education and practice in Europe and America (Somer 2007). In 1928, a group of left-wing Swiss architects declared, "the need for a new concept of architecture that satisfies the spiritual, intellectual and material demands of present day life." (Conrads 1970) For the next thirty years CIAM congresses aligned the objectives of architecture and town planning, promoting its views internationally through an exchange of ideas. Those ideas, intentions and focus developed over time. The three initial 1928 categories of dwelling, producing and relaxation (the maintenance of the species), became four by the time of the 1933 CIAM 4 congress. Housing, work, recreation and transportation captured the theme of the congress, 'The Functional City', although this underwent further iterations into a more structured system of principles for the urban consciousness. This progression took place as a result of the congresses of the 1950s held in Hoddesdon, England in 1951 (CIAM 8), in Aix-en-Provence, France in 1953 (CIAM 9) and in Dubrovnic, Yugoslavia in 1956 (CIAM 10).

Arguably, the main events which brought urban consciousness and issues of the city to the forefront in both the practical and academic worlds, can be traced back to as early as 1943 with José Luis Sert's publication, Can our cities survive?: an abc of urban problems, their analysis, their solutions. This was followed in 1951 by the theme, The Heart of the City, formulated by the CIAM 8. The congress publication The Heart of the City: towards the humanization of urban life, initiated a new approach to urban planning challenging the four categories of 'The Functional City' with 'The Cores within the Urban Constellation'. (Mumford 2007)

Ultimately, CIAM 10 expanded the theme of Heart of the City, promoting an "architecture that takes the urban possibilities into consideration. It counts on the environment". (Mumford 2009) With these words, Sert, acting as secretary of the CIAM 10 openly contrasted the functionalist model of the l'Unite' d'Habitation with a new urban model he was testing in the South American cities "... with high blocks alternating with lower structures and courts ... with shops and public to other more specific categories such as "house, street, district and city", the focus shifted to "social interaction, community and habitat". (Mumford 2000)

CIAM participants defined habitat as "the locality in which an animal naturally grows and lives" and sits comfortably with the historical framework of Venice. This definition, however, was a broader and deeper expression of urbanistic fundamentals, and came to formulate a new concept of architectonic and urbanistic means. Consequently, it envisaged a greater responsibility for the future of the city and an active role for the new figure of the architect-urbanist. By displaying 35 analytical grids as the schematic method of analysis or "thinking tool" the participants to the CIAM 10, compared the current urban problems to that time in their respective countries, formalizing the ambitious theme of a new Charte de l'Habitat. (Mumford 2000)

And what of the CIAM Schools, activities that ran in parallel to all of the 1950s CIAM congresses? Venice hosted the one month long CIAM School testing in 1952 within its ground current architectonic and urbanistic themes of Mobility. The following year it held another school, Historic Centre as the centre of touristic and cultural activities, and in 1954 the New gateway to the historic centre, and finally in 1956, New developments in the mainland. Both lecturers and students discussed themes of urban architecture using the same methodology of the analytical grids from the CIAM congresses.

As a point of interest for the Venice-Sydney collaboration, the architect Phillip Jackson was one of two delegates from Sydney who actively contributed to the CIAM 10 debate and attended the CIAM School in Venice. (McKay, Jackson 1957) Jackson went on to test this 'architect-urbanist' model, his point of reference being his contribution to Harry Seidler's controversial and unrealized 1957 project for McMahon's Point in North Sydney. The architects and planners involved in the project rose to the challenge in their landmark re-development study proposal "Urban Redevelopment Concerns You!" Ultimately, the proposal failed to realize aspirations for innovative high-density urban/architecture, apart from isolated gestures such as Seidler's Blues Point Tower, completed in 1962. Notwithstanding, by locating the theoretical roots of McMahon's Point in the 1956 CIAM congress, we can re-assess the role of the CIAM in what was an emerging discourse on the new element of urban consciousness that challenged architects, landscape architects and planners to adopt urbanistic means. (Favaro 2014)

With an article written by the young architect Gino Valle, a local architecture journal introduced the first CIAM School in Venice as the post-graduate architecture summer course, suggesting:

> Venezia rappresenta un terreno ideale di esperienza e arricchimento per l'architettura e la scienza urbanistica: citta' che si raggruppa con un organismo unico in una scala squisitamente umana. Venezia e' si un caso particolare ma appunto per questa sua unicita' e la polarizzazione dei suoi problemi nel settore umano, puo' provocare piu' valide e profonde reazioni nello studente. (Gino Valle 1952)

Needless to say, the CIAM Summer Schools were an extraordinary and rich design experience, with Venice being fertile ground for reflection about habitat, human scale, as well as the ideal terrain for experiments and enrichments in architettura e urbanistica. During the CIAM School in 1956, Italian architects like Franco Albini, Giancarlo De Carlo and Ludovico Quaroni, to name the most well-known, reinforced Le Corbusier's praise of Venice as an organizing system, which he developed further in his address to the CIAM School in 1952. (CIAM School 1956) They discussed the role of the architect-urbanist as part of a planning community rather than the individual professional in charge of directing design solutions (Albini), the dialectic relationship between design principles and planning instruments and how the action of the urbanist begins from existing realities (De Carlo) and urbanistica conceived as planning, programming and action all referred to the spaces of human activity regulated by political and administrative choices (Quaroni). The CIAM debates and the CIAM Schools in Venice contributed to the reading of Venice as an integrated system of urban architecture in some way abandoning previous reading of Venice renaissance splendor and theatrical image.

Imago

Many historians and critics of architecture have observed and celebrated the image of Venice through the descriptions of its splendid churches as well as of its private and public palaces. So, what is the significance of this?

A comparison might be drawn here about two distinct periods of Venice: one set in the past during the renaissance time and one set now in the contemporary time. In the 1980s two historians of architecture Manfredo Tafuri and Colin Rowe made two insightful observations about Venice and the Renaissance. The comparison aims to assist this chapter in clarifying Le Corbusier's proposition and examining the recent contemporary architecture with some thoughts in discerning what would be the future of Venice. Interestingly, through a different approach, one more political the other one driven more by formal descriptions, Tafuri and Rowe both came to the conclusion that in the sixteenth century the political or architectural debate in Venice was about the strive for an imago of the city. Tafuri's very illuminating volume Venice and the Renaissance described the political position of a group of Venetian Patriciates called the *primi* who for Tafuri were the real protagonists of the Renaissance story. Their dream was to renew the city not just with renovations and restructures of the old buildings rather with the realization of new buildings for a new image of the city. And to realize new buildings they led the political institutions of the Senate and the Council of Ten to call upon the professional figure of the architect to give a new image to Venice. The vision was to develop Venice as the new Rome and compete with the other European capitals. How was the Repubblica Serenissima (The most Serene Republic) ready to achieve that? The answer to this question can be found in the government of the city that set up three political figures or groups: first a public commission called Savi al Comodo e all'Ornato which translates as advisers concerned with the serviceable and the beautiful, the Council of Ten who for example commissioned the architect Michele Sanmicheli to draw an overall plan for the defense of Venice and the proto or public architect who was responsible for major and complex urban projects. Thus, Jacopo Sansovino was appointed for the urban design and transformation of Piazza San Marco and the Basilica di San Marco the central place of both the religious and the political powers and later in 1570 Andrea Palladio became the proto or the public architect of the Serenissima for the design of the Redentore Church and San Giorgio Maggiore. Later in the 1600s, Vincenzo Scamozzi was called for the design of the Procuratie Nuove, the last significant addition realized in Piazza San Marco.

Thus Jacopo Sansovino, Andrea Palladio and Vincenzo Scamozzi conceived and expressed the new image of Venice with palaces and churches realized in dominant and strategic positions across the city and the lagoon. In Piazza San Marco, in Giudecca Island, in San Giorgio Island these architects contributed to increase the number of great visible urban architectures therefore to expand the tendency of Venice of being a Theatrical City. This is on the other hand Colin Rowe's reading of Venice as a theatrical city composed by 'self-sufficient neighborhoods' or insulae. With each insula providing a series of spatial theatrical ambiances defined by the key visible elements of its urban architecture. Thus, Venice urban architecture can be interpreted as a "polyphonic system" – a term borrowed from Massimo Cacciari - where arguably the three systems of movement, activities and visibility were three of the main ingredients for an urban architecture model city to be copied into the future.

In current times and with the assistance of government figures and institutions including the City Council, the Sovrintendenza alle Belle Arti, the Biennale and private fondazioni such as Pinault and Prada, the professional figure of the proto has been called up again. Is that reasonable to say that the political circumstances might be similar to the renaissance times but the realizations are very different?

New Realizations
Renata Codello's (2014) Contemporary Architecture in Venice, as the title suggests, presents an overview of Venice's major pieces of contemporary architecture over the last 20 years. The book confirms and recognizes the modernity of this city, based if nothing else on the large number of recently realized projects built in Venice. From 2006, Codello is the superintendent of the Soprintendenza per i beni architettonici e paesaggistici di Venezia e Laguna. As part of the governing body of the City she has been instrumental in facilitating the design and realization of many new buildings and in the period between

2005-2010 together with academic and mayor of Venice Massimo Cacciari. Through their influential role Codello and Cacciari have successfully completed a number of projects within the city's historic centre and on the island of Giudecca. Codello's publication, with an introduction of Cacciari, is a reflection on that period. In that sense Codelli and Cacciari, almost denying the myth of Venice of being the city per excellence of conservative preservation, typified by the unreliazed modernist projects designed by F.L.Wright (Palazzina Maser on the Grand Canal, 1953), Le Corbusier (San Giobbe Hospital, 1964), and Louis Khan (Conference centre and exhibition hall at the Biennale Giardini, 1968) have participated to the realization of a number of complex and innovative contemporary architecture documented in the book. So, what did Venice learn from this missed opportunity, from three un-built projects which could have given Venice a new modernist direction?

And how does the contemporary architecture fit within the historic city?

The answer is in Codello's and Cacciari's book: the twenty years of realized projects, which mystify the 1950s-1960s not yet forgotten unrealized projects.

The intention of these new interventions was to make them emerge from the "organic whole" to facilitate the movement through the city, revitalize great 'modern' industrial buildings into residential in particular at the Giudecca island, redevelop public institutions into cultural activities like at the Punta della Dogana and finally make a point of distinction to promote Venice as a modern city.

And the diversity here stands clearly in the realized projects themselves as documented by Codello. By contrast, they are not as visible and in critical strategic positions as the buildings realized in the renaissance time. By focusing primarily on interior adaptations, renovations and reuse of existing architectures, the new 'constructions' are weaved within the Venetian urban fabric fostering invisibility to the daily visitor. With a few visible projects realised for the new imago of Venice in particular in the movement system with the new Ponte della Costituzione (Santiago Calatrava's new bridge, 2008), and the People Mover (Francesco Cocco's light monorail, 2010) most of the other projects are very much confined inside the historical buildings of Ca' Pesaro (Boris Podrecca, 2002), Gran Teatro La Fenice (Aldo Rossi, 2003), Santa Marta Church (Vittorio De Feo, 2006), the Arsenale (Alberto Cecchetto, 2009), Punta della Dogana (Tadao Ando, 2009), Fondazione Vedova at the Zattere (Renzo

Piano, 2009), Teatrino Grassi (Tadao Ando, 2013), Fondazione Querini Stampalia (Mario Botta, 2013), and at the Gallerie dell'Accademia (Tobia Scarpa and Renata Codello, 2013). The significance of this argument is that it questions if there still room in Venice for delivering completely new projects of the same caliber as the renaissance work or if the new constructions might follow Le Corbusier's ordering system and design tool he employed for the unrealized Venice Hospital. The ordering system of movement and activity within the Campo and the Insula can be found in the recent residential projects by Gino Valle (social housing ex- area Trevisan, 1986), Vittorio Gregotti (ex-Saffa Development in San Giobbe, 1981) or in the Giudecca island with Cino Zucchi project (area ex-Junghans, 2003), Alvaro Siza (Campo di Marte, 2008) second stage project initiated by Carlo Aymonino and Aldo Rossi or like the Cittadella della Giustizia (Iginio Cappai, Pietro Mainardi, 2013).

Also one of the most recent buildings, Cappai's & Mainardi's Court of Justice Cittadella della Giustizia (2013) exemplify the typical urban architecture by utilizing a number of existing buildings of the industrial Tobacco factory and playing the role of gateway from Piazzale Roma. But as the new intervention has been completed sandwiched between other two buildings as narrow and enclosed and realized in a material like copper it comes across as a subdue almost invisible architecture. Although the contemporary buildings have interpreted the venetian urban architecture, they all set back from the main circulation system and strategic visible positions within the south edge of Giudecca Island or of San Giobbe in some way reinforcing le Corbusier's design principles of 'organization' and 'ordering system' shifting the attention from 'imagery and 'shape-making'.

Conclusion

In conclusion, thinking about Venice as a modern city and the model for the city in the future, requires a historical framework, one that holds together Venice as the original place for realizing urban architecture through its self-contained insulae or neighborhoods, Venice as the Renaissance city pursuing a new imago through its appointed proto or public architect, Venice as the city per excellence where the past lives comfortably with the present and at the same time allows new systems of movement, activities and visibilities/invisibilities to take place. It is a framework created by such a complex and rich history that produced and will produce again in the future a new kind of theatrical spaces as in Colin Rowe's reading of the city designed to enrich either established structures or develop new urban architectures.

Following these propositions, the students engaged with the Venice Studio 2014 were actively studying, analyzing and experiencing the urban architecture of the existing insulae with the aim of offering a new urban architecture for the un-renovated and disused ex ItalGas gasometro site in Santa Marta. By challenging 'movement' with the design of the new light rail and station, 'activity' with new residential and cultural activities and visibility with the new construction of landmark buildings and/or invisibility with the adaptation of the existing underused circular Gas Tanks, six groups of students engaged with the problematic and the vision for the future of Venice learning to appreciate it as a model for a modern city of the future.

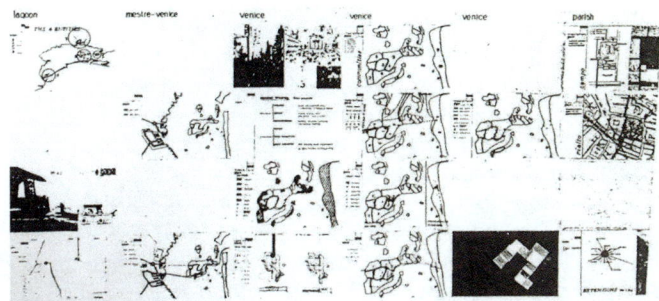

Student research on the theme of The Relationship between Venice and the mainland, 1952 Venice CIAM School

REFERENCES

Leonardo Benevolo with D'Agostino, R. & Toniolo, M., *Quale Venezia. Trasformazioni Urbane 1995-2005*, Marsilio, Venice (2007)

Renata Codello, *Architetture Contemporanee a Venezia*, Fondazione di Venezia, Marsilio (2014)

Ulrich Conrads, *Programs and Manifestoes on 20th-century Architecture*, The MIT Press: Cambridge, Massachusetts, (1970)

Paola Favaro, McMahon's Point, *Sydney: a translation of the 1956 CIAM 10 urban consciousness?* SAHANZ conference 2014, Auckland, New Zealand.

Franco Mancuso, *Venezia è una città – come è stata costruita e come vive*, Corte del Fontego, Venice (2009)

Ian McKay, Philip Jackson, "The 10th C.I.A.M. Conference." *Architecture in Australia*, Volume 46, no.3 (1957)

Eric Mumford, *The CIAM Discourse on Urbanism, 1928-1960*, The MIT Press: Cambridge, Massachusetts (2000)

Eric Mumford, "The Emergence of Mat or Field Buildings" in Sarkis H. *The Corbusier's Venice Hospital* (2001)

Eric Mumford, *Defining Urban Design CIAM Architects and the Formation of a Discipline*, 1937-69, Yale (2009)

Giandomenico Romanelli, *Venezia Ottocento. Materiali per una Storia architettonico e urbanistica della citta' nel XIX secolo*, Officina, Rome (1977)

Colin Rowe, "The most serene republic: Opulence and retardation" in Colin Rowe & Leo Satkowsky, *Italian Architecture of the 16th Century*, Princeton Architectural Press, New York (2002)

Hashim Sarkis, *The Corbusier's Venice Hospital*, Prestel Harvard University Graduate School of Design (2001)

Kees Somer, *The Functional City: CIAM and the Legacy of Van Esteren*, Rotterdam: NAi Publishers (2001)

Manfredo Tafuri, *Venice and the Renaissance*, MIT Press, Cambridge, Mass. (1989).

Gino Valle, *Il Collegamento Venezia-Terraferma tema per il CIAM*, CIAM Schools IUAV Archives (1952)

Katrina Simon

On Immersion As An Architectural Strategy

Venice as a city is at the same time entirely over-familiar and entirely strange. Images of its gleaming monuments rising out of the sea are instantly recognizable from paintings, photographs and films. Any student of art and of design - architecture, landscape architecture, interior architecture, urbanism – has been exposed to its distinctive buildings and characteristic maze-like urban spaces through multiple descriptive and analytical representations. Arriving at the city either by land or sea created for me the shock of recognition experienced in all famous cities, but here made all the more extreme because it was matched with a realization that the familiar images had never seemed quite believable, but were in fact describing a mesmerizing tangible reality.
How can a place so instantly recognizable, yet also so atypical, be used as a laboratory for exploring the possibilities of urban transformation? And how can this be done in a way that transcends the highly idiosyncratic qualities of this city, and allows its experimental possibilities to reflect on wider issues of urban change, for students from very different environments? The Venice Gateway studio structure deployed the strategy of exploring the six sestieri of the city in order to understand how a set of urban relationships and elements came together each of the sestieri in a unique constellation of public places for gathering, for ritual, for commerce and for habitation. This combination provided a set of moves to propose the re-inhabitation of the currently disused site at the edge of the port area as a new gateway for the city.

This process has the benefit of being both analytical and generative as it transfers the discoveries of the form and formation of the existing city to the new location. This form is intricately linked to human life – the need to fresh collect water led to the arrangement and design of the campo that is the social and organizational centre of the urban structure of the islands. While these six patterns of urban living each provided a generative motor for each of the projects, this chapter reflects on six other qualities and dimensions encountered in Venice that offer a powerful inspiration and source of exploration for emerging designers. These derive from the city's setting and history, and are evident at different scales and in different seasons.

The pedagogy of travelling studios emphasizes the rich potential of travel, exposure to different cultures and places, exchanges of life experience between students from different backgrounds and institutions. In Venice, the opportunity arises not just from the profound architectural and landscape history embedded in the city but also from the remarkable ephemeral qualities that emerge from the construction and consolidation

of this history. Even a short time immersed in this environment gives some access to this material and experiential repertoire – less a constellation of urban elements than a vivid trace of their continual emergence, inhabitation and transformation.

Saturation

Two other-worldy creatures appear in a wall, while a third apparition makes its way up through the ground, in an uncompleted section of the cemetery. Saturation has a physical and almost living presence in this city built in the sea. It is present as water, as dampness, as mist. It inhabits surfaces and the depths of materials, revealing the porosity of materials we might otherwise assume to be solid and impervious. It changes as the days and seasons cycle. Its presence leaves a trace in the surfaces of walls and floors and ceilings, marking its advance and retreat, ebb and flow.

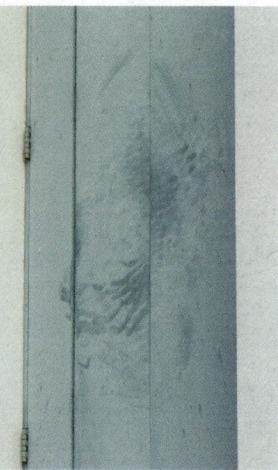

Iteration

Ghostly fingers trace a feathery patina in the zinc cladding of an apartment as they repeatedly reach out and, in a simple but emphatic gesture, pull them closed. This building in Giudeca, designed by Cino Zucci, is just over a decade old, yet it already shows the signs of habit and habitation. These traces of the rituals of daily life are evident everywhere when walking around the city. Patination reveals repetition.

Erasure

Hundreds of bridges link the islets of the city. The underside of the Rialto Bridge shows the wear of water and the scraping of vessels riding along its surface. The brick coursing almost seems to disappear as tiny particles gather in its cracks – its orderly structure apparently erased by wear. The city wears the marks of its continual erosion and erasure. But eroded material also migrates and gathers elsewhere.

Accumulation

As material is erased and eroded it accumulates elsewhere, perhaps in another form. The islands themselves are an accumulation of the sediment in the lagoon, constantly changing shape until fixed by foundations and structures. Life within these structures also causes things to gather – here in David Chipperfield's extension on the cemetery island, watering cans gather for the ritual of tending graves. The city is an accumulation of accumulations – some enduring for hundreds of years, others together just for a morning.

Superimposition

A gap opens up in a wall as bricks settle in uneven and slowly shifting ground. The plaster over the gap has itself cracked, as the ground continues to move, even slightly. The wall and the ground are in a kind of slow dance, and the menders of the wall are also engaged in this performance, plastering over the gap as it widens, and no doubt re-plastering it again when the crack in the plaster ceases to reassure that this addition has the dissolution of the wall under control. The city is layered with such superimpositions – masking, joining, transforming.

Fragmentation

This ancient weathered head-like stone sits high above the Piazza San Marco. In its disintegrating state the processes of sedimentation that made the stone from which it is carved is now becoming apparent as the fissures and layers of its sea-origin are again revealed by erosion. Signs of fragmentation are all around when walking through the city. Here the fragmentation of the stone appears to have been accelerated as the stone has been carved and installed out of its bedding plane – perhaps rotated perpendicular by the immense and immensely slow forces of tectonic movement.

It is the human life span that we use to judge the permanence and durability of materials like stone, when in fact the rock cycle is as enduring and relentless as the hydrological cycle, and minerals move endlessly from sedimentary to metamorphic to volcanic rock. The visible fragmentation of the very fabric of the city is a powerful reminder of this deep cycle of creativity and destruction. The deliberateness with which it has been re-cemented into the balustrade speaks of a care for the stone at every part of its journey as part of the city.

Immersion – In Conclusion

On first arriving in the city it is easy to be overwhelmed by the apparent similarity of each part – each new campo looks slightly familiar and similar. Equally strange is the rapidity with which it becomes possible to trace a route through the city, noting and storing more details than are perhaps conscious. Part of this is a sense of increasing awareness of the minute and intricate variation that is part of the city fabric - not just the already astounding variety of architectural elements large and small from which each sestieri is uniquely composed, but also the distinctive and infinitely varied patterns of water as it saturates stone and wood, of erasure, of accumulation, superimposition and of fragmentation.

Immersion in this mutable environment is an immensely engaging and stimulating experience. It induces a sensitivity to minute changes in materials, to subtle alterations in the way they are connected and altered by the repeated cycles of the environment and of the rituals of ceremonial and daily life. Architecture, landscape architecture and interior architecture are profoundly enriched by this encounter.

All photos by Katrina Simon, Venice, November 2014

Permanence and Change in the Historic City

Anna-Paola Pola

Why does Venice still fascinates us?
Is it the exceptional nature of its waterways, the recognizability of its forms, the uniformity of materials, the poetry of colors, the textured reflections of light and water...?
Sure, but I think there's more.
I think it's the idea of an invention of a city like no other. The idea that a population on the run may reach the brackish water of the lagoon and foresee a new city in a place where there was almost nothing, not even the ground.
The inhabitants of the Veneto plain, to escape the incursions of the barbarians who entered Italy by the Julian Alps, took refuge in the lagoon between the mouth of the River Po and the Tagliamento, a safe environment protected by land and sea.
The poor accessibility of this site and its narrow channels, which allowed circulation only possible by boat, ensured their safety.
Its marginal position compared to the mainland, crossed by invaders over the centuries and agitated by numerous political setbacks, encouraged the independence of the inhabitants. The lack of resources pushed these towards the sea and to the trade. The environmental difficulties stimulated an initiative for the feeling of belonging and a sense of community.
Venice was born this way, and because of this nature it can escape domination from mainland kingdoms, it can become the commercial center between the East and the West and it can find and start its own autonomous political organization. (Benevolo 1975)
The city was founded in a dark time in history thanks to a paradoxical intervention of men who wanted to turn an exceptional environment into a human habitat.
I like to think it is the power of this insane and positivist vision that, in an unconscious and instinctive way, still fascinates us.

An Invention of City

Venice is a total invention and the term *invention* is here to be taken in its proper, ontological sense, as it rarely happens in the history of the city.
This urban creation in the lagoon started from almost nothing. Except for a few outcrop (Dorsoduro) or rare small islets, there was nothing, not even the ground. To proceed with the city development, a necessary step had to be taken, that was, the creation of the land on which to build. So the work continued with a series of little progress and some achievements from the lagoon: drainage, reclaim, piling ...
Even the channels, except for the Grand Canal that gives the general shape to the whole urban area, are not a stable element of the landscape. Some are dry, others are opened in drained areas, the whole system is constantly shaped and reshaped. It thus requires an intense and continuous industry, but also ingenious solutions, imaginative techniques put to work in the various construction sites.
Venice was gradually built with the accumulation of these efforts. (Crouzet-Pavan 1997)
As a complete human creation, the city should also be maintained through continuous men's work, their presence and their daily work support its fragile physical setting.
The city is the product of the constant, gentle and always changeable adaptation of itself in the lagoon. Venice exists as a continuous human enterprise and escapes from time consumption thanks to its indefinitely ability to renew.
The city was built in a relatively short period, between 800 and 1200, however, due to the lack of land for growth and because of the rapid obsolescence of the buildings, since then the buildings transformations have followed with intensity and urban planning has developed through a slow, but continuous and widespread process of consolidation, extension and suture. (Bellavitis 1980)

The Venetian lagoon

The Historic Town

Venice, therefore, continuously renews itself and is passed down in time.
This isn't a traditional old town to expand and transform, but an historic city which has transformed itself several times, there is no building, church or palace in existence today that is not the result of successive transformations and the new projects are often the result of the recycling of the existing urban fabric. (Mancuso 2009)
Hence the exceptional nature of the debate about the intervention methods to be adopted for the project, the protection, the renewal and the restoration of the city and its specific *historic nature*.

During the 1800 the planned interventions projects in the city represented the idea, then in vogue, of the safeguarding as purely physical protection of historic centers intended only as a set of isolated monuments.
Paradoxically, the first restoration experiences were accompanied by destruction. Emblematic was the fate of the Fondaco dei Turchi restored in 1860 according to the romantic criteria that tends to recreate buildings very different from the original. (Bandiani 1978)
Then, just a few years later, on the 14th of July 1902 at 9.52 the San Marco tower bell collapssed.
The same evening, the City Council decided that the bell should be risen "as it was and where it was".
With the bell collapsing the debate on reconstruction was ekindled. This time, however, the reconstruction was conducted with a philological and technical seriousness, publishing all acts in concern, choosing the suitable bricks and stones on the basis of reliable documents, for a historically documented reconstruction. The enterprise ended on the 31st of December 1911.
What prevails is not the aesthetic judgment, but the ethical need to affirm the historical continuity of the city. (Bellavitis 1980)
The "as it was and where it was" became an intervention model so famous that today it is an expression cited around the world in Italian, its original language, "com'era e dov'era".
It is Piero Gazzola who sealed this formula with the reconstruction of the Verona bridge after the Second World War.

Piazza San Marco with the rubble of the collapsed bell tower, photo by Aldo Jesurum.

NEXT PAGE: Commemorative stamps issued for the inauguration of the tower rebuilt, April 25, 1912, drawings by Augusto Sezanne.

Piero Gazzola was a superintendent of the Veneto region after the war. He promoted Venice in the Second International Congress of Architects and Technicians of Historic Monuments from the 25th to the 31st of May 1964. During this encounter a document was defined and is now considered the basis of contemporary thought on urban conservation: the Venice Charter.

The document was written with the intent to establish a code of international guidelines for the conservation and restoration of monuments, architectures and historical sites.

Here, for the first time, it was stated that the notion of monument includes not only the architectural works, but also the human environment and the landscape and that the monument conservation is not inseparable from its environment.

In these years the idea emerged that it is the entire environment to create the mood of the city, therefore, " not only the individual monuments taken one by one should be conserved, but rather the whole environment in which they live", the houses, the gardens, the views ... are these "essential elements that give the scale of the monumental works" according to a good expression used in 1958 by the Italian architect Luigi Piccinato in the report for the master plan of the city of Bursa in Turkey. (Piccinato 1977)

The modern policies regarding urban conservation are based on this principle, that is, the acknowledgement of the historical value of the urban fabric, the understanding of its structure and form, and the analysis of the complex layering process that generated them. (Bandarin 2012)

The Project for the Existing City

Using a past trace in the present (in the form of narrative, memory, document or monument) as a basis of comparison for the project's future is tied to the idea of progress, and the preservation of the past as a tool for designing an ever transforming present is certainly a modern invention.

It is above all after the experience of World War II that matures in the urban culture an original idea for the city, which saw in the need for conservation the condition for the cultural balance of land and society. (Magrin 2015)

After World War II Italy was the training ground of this idea and Venice, with its unique historic setting and its international role, was one of the privileged places for this debate, in fact sealed with the Charter named after the city.

The historical centers in Italy form a large proportion of the housing stock and at the same time a heritage of incomparable value.

The identification of a specific process, of analysis and operational intervention in the town historic areas, developed in Italy during the sixties with the aim to preserve and restore the historic urban core, consolidated before the industrial revolution and interpreted as a unified body, made of buildings, open spaces and inhabitants.This thought comes as a reaction to the plans of thinning and demolition, it is the result of the debate on the reconstruction of war-ravaged Italian towns and takes shape after the great economic development connected to post-war modernization.

The operating process is outlined in case after case, specializing in the practice of urban design and action plans of cities such as Bologna, Brescia, Urbino, Venice, Palermo ...

Leonardo Benevolo, professor of history of architecture in Venice between 1963 and '71, well described this method.

First of all, the object of conservation is redefined, that is, it's not just a set of physical artifacts - monuments and works of art, protected in the name of a specialized interest, historical or artistic - but an inhabited organism, characterized by a high quality space that is generally felt to be missing in the contemporary city yet is still required according to a modern urban research.

It has been clear right from the very first experiments that to really maintain this system, you need to operate on the whole city, even on the metropolitan area, because here lies the conceptual, functional and social space to understand, accept and organize the ancient city.

Then the original building fabric must be studied and restored, distinguishing the types of buildings - palaces, houses, churches, convents, special buildings, green spaces, etc. - to be able to determine the possible use and the eligible operations to adapt to each type of buildings.

In the parts already altered adjacent the old town, the potential empty spaces are retrieved for the bulkier facilities that are not in the ancient spaces. In the suburbs, the growth should be limited and arrested, gradually directing the public and private initiatives towards the rehabilitation of existing assets.

In the mid-70s the urgency of the problems and the Italian example developed a general awareness of the need to preserve the ancient heritage.

In 1972 UNESCO promoted several projects of urban conservation throughout Europe during the Intergovernmental Conference on Cultural Policies in Europe.

In 1975 the Council of Europe declared the European Year of Architectural Heritage. At this first opportunity to internationally debate about these topics, architects, planners and administrators confronted on 50 cases of study examples made in 17 different

Planned transformation in the historical city, Venice master plan by L. Benevolo 1996

- residential before '800
- residential before '800
- residential '800
- special building before '800
- special building '800
- others building before '800
- others building '800/'900
- private green
- public green
- interventions: restoration
- interventions: new buildings
- interventions: renovation for new uses

countries. In a few years these shared experiences helped ensure that this type of intervention on historic towns was to become an established practice throughout Europe. The didactic strength of the Italian examples conducted these experiences and the national debates beyond Europe itself. The intervention model for the project and the protection of the historic city was exported everywhere, and is widely regarded as the most important Italian contribution to modern international architectural research. (Benevolo 1960)

The City of Heritage

Today the world's changed perception, as a result to the globalization phenomena, is perhaps one of the reasons why there is a renewed interest in the issues concerning the protection of the ancient city. Nowadays, the conservation of historic centers is still discussed a lot, or more generally the conservation of urban areas. Projects and studies are proposed for the conservation of places that are culturally or geographically distant from Europe.

But the question related to the protection of the existing city is often ambiguous: today we talk about conservation misusing words like identity, values, heritage, terms probably never used in the experiences elected as a reference model and from which the debate was launched.

As for the contemporary cities and societies, sometimes - more and more often - an invention of tradition is proposed that, in the absence of urban knowledge and consciousness, easily leans on an inadequate or inconsistent image, exposing itself to new forms of speculation. (Magrin 2015)

The city conservation project was a much needed project formed as a cultural response to a planning problem which even today remains largely unresolved and is actually amplified by the social and environmental global emergencies.

If you look from a distance at the point where the city conservation project started, our actuality appears almost paradoxical: the collective consciousness seems to have effectively accepted the reasons and opportunities also cultural for the historic city and landscape conservation, the institutions often take charge of these issues. Where this does not happen, the international organizations pressed by the community respond with effective interventions.

But the urban conservation project has not been completed and the historical centers, although protected, remain an urban problem. The habit of conservation, the normalization of protection within the systems of rules and established and shared practices, not always provide convincing answers to the basic question: Why conserve?

It is a question that by its nature, constantly interrogates the present, and because of this it needs answers continuously renewed.
Francesco Bandarin and Ron van Oers in their book *Historic Urban Landscape* propose a revealing dilemma between Venice and Varanasi.
They say Venice is today the most famous example of an historic city that has been preserved in its full physical authenticity, but, at the same time, it exemplifies the almost complete loss of social and cultural values, clearly reflected in the out-migration and substitution of most of the population, and in the dominance of the tourism as the unic economic activity. In this sense, Venice is an international iconic heritage image, but it has not been preserved as an historic urban entity.
If you consider the socially conscious urban conservation principles, Venice is a failure, however, it is difficult to say that its universal significance has been lost, as it is proven by the unique character of its urban form, the enduring importance of its artistic achievements and by its success as a global centre for tourism and for the arts.
On the contrary Varanasi, venerated city by Hindus, Buddhists, Jains and Senthoo, has remained in the past three millennia as the sacred place for millions of pilgrims. Here, while the traditional values associated with religion and spirituality are authentic and intact, the same cannot be said of the urban and architectural fabric, which has been continuously transformed, destroyed and altered. In spite of the lack of authenticity and physical integrity, the values of Varanasi as an historic city and spiritual centre are totally intact.
So here is the author's dilemma: when choosing the city that best exemplifies our contemporary concept of heritage, should it be Venice or Varanasi? (Bandarin 2012)

The City as an Entail
The historic city has an economic value attributed to the performance of the land budget, to the advantage of the tourists flows and the logistics location. It has also a cognitive value, reported by the different histories, policies, social events, customs, arts and techniques that can be recalled in the historic city.
Today we have to replace the value of the historical hereditary built within the broader and global debate on sustainability and the possibility of action to bequeath to future generations. It is clear that the preservation of the historic town is the first step towards a sustainable vision of the city.
Designing within a historic city means defining the spatial configuration of the city, understanding the roles that are employed within the urban and metropolitan context, measuring it on the hosting functions, building a new figure consistent with what the center is and

still means: a bequest, a deposit of incessant things that human activity has left in that place at the time of the first settlement.

It is not right for a vital city to freeze its structures: it is because the city was made out of space and historically stratified construction, techniques and symbol, we must accept the changing rule as a condition for the city life.

In the historic city what assiduously changes are contents, lives and deeds of the people, while *things* show more inertia although inevitably they also end up to be determined. So we have to find a method of intervention that is compatible with the necessary terms "permanence and change". (Macchi Cassia 1980)

The Milanese architect Ernesto N. Rogers argued that to preserve or to build are moments of the same act of consciousness, and do not make sense if not in the sense of actualization of the past and continuation of the historical process. (Rogers 1958)

Venice for its nature of a complete artificial construction is based on the functional and on the ongoing verification of this organization to the changing needs.

This means that there has always been a refusal for stillness in the history of the city, because the salvation of the ancient city is realized through its transformation and because "only reinventing the city you can know it deeply." (Macchi Cassia 1980)

REFERECES

E.Bardiani, G.Conti, "Venezia: dalla città speciale al modello di sviluppo speciale", in *Urbanistica* n.68-69 (1978)

F. Bandarin, R. Van Oers, *Historic Urban Landscape*, Wiley-Blackweel (2012)

G. Bellavis, *Venezia*, editoriale Espresso, Roma (1980)

L. Benevolo, *Storia dell'architettura moderna*, Laterza, Roma (1960) 1999

L. Benevolo, *Storia della città. La città medievale*, Roma (1975) 2006

E. Crouzet-Pavan, *Venise: une invention de la ville*, Seyssel (1997)

C. Macchi Cassia, *Relazione del Piano particolareggiato per il centro storico di Melzo*, (1980)

A. Magrin, "La conservazione della città è un problema urbanistico", in *Esportare il centro storico - Exposrting the Urban Core*, Milano (2015)

F. Mancuso, *Venezia è una città*, Venezia (2009)

E. Nathan Rogers, "Verifica culturale dell'azione urbanistica", in *Difesa e valorizzazione del paesaggio urbano e rurale*, Atti del VI Convegno Nazionale di Urbanistica (1958)

L. Piccinato, *Relazioni a Piani Regolatori 1926-1974 1975-1977*, Roma (1977)

Uffici INPS, architect Angelo Scattolin, 1957-63
photo: Tommaso Altamura

Venice in transformation

CONVERSATION with Alberto Cecchetto
Wednesday 10th December 2014 h.15,30
Cotonificio IUAV Venezia

We would like to know your opinion about the idea of Venice as a modern city, from your point of view as an architect, urban planner and academic.
I think that the question does not have only one answer, it has many.
The opposition ancient-modern is in my opinion a warped reading of the reality due to the difficulty of reconciling different languages.
In reality there is not a city more transformed than Venice. Theoretically, Venice is always the same. In reality, the use of the city has radically changed. When I was a child on Sundays we always went to Piazza San Marco. There was the band playing there every Sunday. Now, I never go to the Piazza. Today the city has been expropriated.
Venice is a city that allows people to take photos. Because of that it is untouchable. But if you look in the interior of the buildings, the city has been radically transformed.
On the other hand, however, Venice is perhaps the city where you can better anticipate the future. It is the most modern city in which I have worked.
[A.C. shows his project at the Arsenale in Venice] This is a typical European design theme. In Europe you cannot build the new, simply by demolishing the old. Here in Europe and even more in Venice, the approach is different. You have to work with surgical operations and urban acupuncture within the existing historic tissue of the city. The existing city becomes matter of a design project.
This is why Venice is a perfect workshop. The dialogue between old and new materials is the key to understanding the future project.

I worked in the Arsenale trying to create a language made of dramatic solutions. One of the main efforts has been to capture the light from the roof and bring it inside. The materials used are the cheapest as possible; galvanized steel and chipboard. I created a distance between the old structure and the new solution, to produce a historical awareness. History is not something old and departed. History is what exists now.

I am going to publish a book with my work about Venice. The title of the introduction is "What did I learn from the Arsenal." I am not a historian. I cannot write the history of this place, but I can tell what the place has taught me in terms of architectural design. First thing is that the public space is an incredible opportunity for collective life. We cannot destroy or abandon the attitude of European cities to create spaces where people can meet without a functional defined program. Are we able to re-create spaces that are suitable environments to a community life? Are we able to reclaim this lifestyle?

Another issue is the ability to get an idea for the future. Looking at the Venetian territory from above, one can see how it has been developed without a common project and the current landscape is derived from the summary of small individual solutions, made without having an idea of its future totality. This is a metropolitan area of more than 3 million inhabitants built without the control of the end result. Another lesson that comes from Venice is that reconciliation with the environment is not a problem of technology, but it is a problem of cultural approach. It means to be able to consider water, sun and local materials as the substance of the project.

Italian architects who have trained with my generation have had three myths: first is preservation as absolute principle, second is more rules equal to more quality, third is to consider the reality a little 'dirty' compared to the theory, we are so much idealistic.

From these three myths we should do just the opposite. So I have created three commandments. Frst, conservation does not exist, there is a transformation and architecture is the active participant to that transformation; second, about the rules: simplify; third, we must be a bit more empirical.

Alberto, you talked before about the Arsenal as a perfect place for experimentation, we were wondering if the same can be said about Venice. Is Venice a good workshop for students?

The Arsenal is a perfect laboratory, because it was a place of production, where ships were built. Here there is no style, no decoration, nor ornament, it is not the Ca d'Oro with its flamboyant Gothic, here there are only the essential elements, here there is the rational part of Venice. It was conceived as one large open space of about 250 square meters with 180 columns. Unfortunately, in the Austrian period it has been divided into smaller rooms, which ruined the fluidity of the space. I found myself arguing with the authority because I wanted to recreate that original space. That was not possible.

There was a fig in the impluvium that grew up on the rock. Its roots drew the necessary water from the bricks. I said to the authority that we had to preserve the fig more than the older parts of plaster, because the fig tree was a more important part of the history than the building... they thought I was crazy, I think.

Le Corbusier used to say that Venice is a perfect solution to provide ideas for building the city of the future. Its rules of construction are very rational, democratic, there is hierarchy and cluster together and there is a pedestrian network of paths separate and independent from the water channels, used for the transport of goods.

I think that the future of Venice is centered on the idea that Venice does not exist anymore, but it is part of a larger area that includes the ancient city, the lagoon and the requalification of the semi-abandoned area of the industrial town of Marghera. With eight young collaborators, I am currently working on a book called 'Venice', instead of 'Venezia'. The challenge of this work is to ask if we would be able in the future to build a contemporary city as beautiful as Venice, a city that people will come to see from all over the world.

We are working on a new city on the water in the area of Marghera, with bridges and canals and stained glass windows reflected on the water, we try to think in the same way the Venetians would have thought.

By designing "Venice", I learned to see Marghera with other eyes, not only as an industrial area, with chimneys, oil, pollution ... Even Venice in the past was not a comfortable place, with mud, slime, algae and lack of land where to build.

In Marghera, I apply the same exercise, the same approach. How to build a sustainable city for the future starting from the rules drawn from the Venetian example: separate pedestrian paths, respect for the environment, mixed use of spaces, activities and assets ... That is not easy.

Alberto, you are an architect, urban designer and landscape architect but also a university professor. To what extent is the integration of these disciplines important for you?

It is essential. I am the only teacher in Italy who is professor of both architectural design and city planner. When, with the new law, they told me that I had to choose, I replied that I never choose, because I am an architect. Even Giancarlo De Carlo, who was my teacher, created a series of integrated laboratories teaching architecture and urban design, and I will not give up the integration of these disciplines.

I realized that I have no preconceived languages. De Carlo taught me to keep my eyes open, and the same did Le Corbusier. I remember that during an interview Le Corbusier said that the first thing to teach students is why to open the windows in that point of the facade. The answer is because of the view of the landscape from that specific point. This means that there is never a single solution. This was also the approach of De Carlo, who taught me to be open-minded. He always pushed me to move on, to proceed without stopping on a language or a style.

Design and History

INTERVIEW WITH ALBERTO FERLENGA
Thursday, January 15, 2015, at 18,
study of prof. Ferlenga, Cotton Mill,
IUAV University of Venice

We would like to have your opinion on the role of Venice today as a modern city.
Modernity in Venice, despite what you may think, has always existed. Perhaps, even more than in other places. Venice is not a city without modern buildings, but modernity here has assumed different aspects. In some way the modernity in Venice was cloaked or made-up with forms that were not in our idea of modernity. Much of Venice was vaguely constructed according to gothic forms or other forms that, if we look at when they were built, are in fact a version of modernity, a modernity that maybe we don't like so much, but yet it was modernity at that time.
Then there is the modernity of the projects, the ones that we all know, the ones of Kahn, of Le Corbusier ...
There is the modernity of the interiors, of the details, the refined modernity of Carlo Scarpa.
There is the extreme modernity of Venice outside Venice, in the industrial part of Venice, Marghera.
There is the modernity of the lagoon. The lagoon changes constantly, it does not change by nature, changes continuously because of human projects and these projects are an expression of modernity, maybe not architectural modernity, but the boundaries between infrastructure and architecture are quite blurred boundaries. The ultimate expression of this is the MOSE, a quite controversial project from the political point of view, with all what we know now of corruptions. Yet, one of the largest European works of this type ever built. This is just the latest project of a construction process of the Venetian lagoon that has always been totally artificial. If there was not the modernity in different areas, there would not be the Venetian

lagoon. It was preserved by modern interventions, modern for the time in which they were made. These interventions started in ancient times from the detour of two rivers, and went on with the continuous construction of barriers, defenses, 'murazzi' as we call them ... These define a great modern project.
In my opinion, because of this attitude to continuously modifying itself, modernity in Venice has never been a problem. It produced discussions, as in the case of the last work of Koolhaas in Rialto, but not a rejection. It led to a discussion about the meaning of that work and also about its quality. In my opinion it is not a nice project by Koolhaas, this is the issue, but the fact that that building (Fondaco dei Tedeschi) was greatly transformed over time means that nobody is offended if someone makes a project there, the issue is that it has to be a good project.
Venice is a city that has a good relationship with modernity. Modernity is a fairly broad concept that affects not just the architecture and not just the architecture that looks modern, because there is also a modern architecture, which is not modern, and a modernity that also covers others various field of engineering, infrastructure ...
Compared to this, we must establish that paradoxically Venice, in its historical form, is in some ways the city more embalmed in Italy, but it is also the city that has perhaps been the most dynamic and modern.
Who made an industrial operation so strong in front of an ancient city? Marghera is one of the largest industrial areas in Europe. None has ever made an operation like that, with that strength and with that proximity.
My idea is that Venice is a city, that despite everything, has always had a good relationship with modernity. Maybe today, Venice begins to have a more complicated relationship with it, because of the economical growth of tourism that collects 20-30 million visitors a year. This involves a predetermined idea of what one expects from the city, what tourist expects. Unfortunately, the tourist expects that the city confirm itself. This becomes a problem because to respond to that, the city tends to reproduce his mask rather than developing the dynamism that it has always had.

From the educational point of view, what is the impact of Venice on the students, what can the students still learn from Venice?
The essential problem that Venice offers, especially today, is precisely what was said before, his gradual emergence as a

mask. The problem is that we have to teach what Venice is really, to forget this aspect or at least, we have to teach to exit from the constraints that entail living in a theatrical scene.
Hugo Pratt in his comic books Corto Maltese shows us very well how Venice is full of moments of escape, moments in which the mask falls. The problem is to teach this, that what we mostly see, what it is produced in billions of photographs that are taken in Venice and spread throughout the world is the least interesting part of Venice. Students and tourists must learn how to scratch that habit of looking that it is still very strong. Venice is essentially another thing, this is something that we must teach, because otherwise, it remains only the conservation, that is useless, we don't protect nothing, we just let the city die, we condemn it to its single image, a single image of a time while the city has had many.
I always had difficulty to propose the city where I work as a topic of study for students. I always need a certain distance. But we have worked with international workshops on Marghera, which is a topic typically Venetian. I am personally designing a piece of MOSE around the area of Chioggia (just south of Venice).

Continuing on this aspect of your profession, you are a professor at the IUAV and an architect, how do you see this integration between the professional world and the university?
Particularly in this case of the MOSE in Chioggia, there is an integration between the two worlds. I am working as an architect at the MOSE, but through an agreement with the University. At some point the IUAV of Venice was called to intervene on the architectural parts of that project. I say at some point, because this is the whole crux of the difficulties. Because only when they realized that building such a huge structure in a delicate situation like Venice was perhaps not a brilliant idea, the superintendence, that from this point of view is very careful and very active, has imposed to design also an architectural project.
This experience was very interesting. Venice has always had an important tradition in the construction of infrastructure and in the control of water, also from the aesthetic point of view. The forts were not only forts, often they were made by important personalities of the architectural word, that is, there is always an assumption of responsibility in designing Venice.
Then turn an engineering project in something that would deal with a particular landscape and could also constitute a design occasion for the city was a very important thing.
The contact between the professional world and the universi-

ties is not easy in Italy, because the university is quite hostile to the outside world. In our best architectural moments we were able to bring together the design aspects with historical and theoretical aspects. In other cultures this has not occurred, but in Italy and especially in this School of Venice, in some happy moments this happened. Aldo Rossi with his book 'The architecture of the city', is an example of how an architect builds the theory on which to base his work, and this was an example followed by other important architect like Venturi in 'Learning from Las Vegas', Colin Rowe in 'Collage city' until recently by Rhem Koolhaas in 'Delirious New York'.

Urban Survey and Design

Aerial view of Venice
From its beginning (between 600 to 800 a.c.), Venice had developed an urban system that reproduces the model of the morphological and typological gothic lot system, but due to its geographical location in the mid of a large lagoon the final result was the creation of an urban settlement very different to other European cities. Based on the organic growth of individual cells/nucleus called *insulae* that is, small islands, which slowly enlarged to become larger *insulae* reducing the water spaces between them, the main concept of Venice is in fact in the relation between the land space and the water space.
More *insulae* linked together, each of them developed around a civil and religious main space, with some important settlements also of religious orders, creating a larger neighbourhood. Venice was subdivided in six parts, called *Sestieri* - that is, six neighbourhoods, which students discovered while analysing the city. These are: Santa Croce, Dorsoduro, San Polo, Cannareggio, San Marco, Castello. Each *insula* within its *sestiere* has a specific morphology, a recognizable urban configuration that is the result of medieval, renaissance, baroque, Napoleonic, Austrian, Italian, industrial, modern and more contemporary transformations from its initial period identified between the last centuries of the first millennium and the XIV century.

The urban elements of the city of Venice have unique names that are to be found only in Venice:
- Calli are the small streets between two sides of buildings.
In Venice there are only two roads called "via"- these are: Via Garibaldi in the Castello neighbourhood and Via XXII Marzo in the San Marco neighbourhood; and one road, called "strada":

Strada Nuova in the Cannaregio neighbourhood.
- All other routes are called *calli, ruga* (large street with shops on both sides) *or ramo* (which literally means branch and is a short street that sometimes ends in the canal).
- The *fondamenta* is a street along a canal; the *salizada* is a large and more important street usually paved, the *riva* is a street along a canal and the lagoon. For example: *riva degli Schiavoni* in San Marco.
- There is only one square, which is *Piazza* San Marco; the other large meeting places are called *Campo* or *Campiello* if it is smaller and *Corte* (courtyard). *Campo* means field and this name originates from the notion that these areas once were green fields.
- There are only three Canals – these are, *Canal Grande, Canale Di Cannareggio and Canale della Giudecca* - all the other canals are called *Rio*.
- *Rio tera' (Interrato)* is a canal which has been closed and transformed into a calle.
- There are only four bridges which cross the Canal Grande. These are: *il Ponte della Ferrovia, il Ponte di Rialto e il Ponte dell' Accademia* and the most recent *il Ponte della Costituzione,* which links *Piazzale Roma* (with a car park) with the *Ferrovia* (the railway station), designed by the Spanish architect Santiago Calatrava and opened in 2008.
- The *imbarcadero* is the landing stage/pier/jetty on *the fondamenta* where the *vaporetto* (that means waterbus or ferry) lands.

Urban survey

The first activity to be realized in the first two days of the workshop was a morphological analysis of a typical insula of the historic centre of Venice. Divided in six groups, one for each *Sestiere*, students were invited to study the urban morphology of an *insula* as part of their selected *Sestiere*. Tracing the relation between solid and voids, each group drew the figure ground of the interior and exterior spaces. Through individual and group experiences walking through the site, researching and analysing selected documentation, students represented one part of an insula to include the expertise of each discipline: the hierarchy and shape of the *calli,* the form and function of the main open spaces, the *campo*, the architectural volume and spatial ambiance, the intimate interior spaces of specific public or religious buildings, commercial and private habitation and their relationship with the constructed urban landscape of the *campo*.

Each group was assigned one Insula and one Campo from the six sestieri as listed below:
Group 1. Sestiere Santa Croce with Campo San Giacomo dell'Orio
Group 2. Sestiere Dorsoduro with Campo Santa Margherita
Group 3. Sestiere San Polo with Campo della Pescheria (in Rialto)
Group 4. Sestiere Cannaregio with Campo Madonna dell' Orto

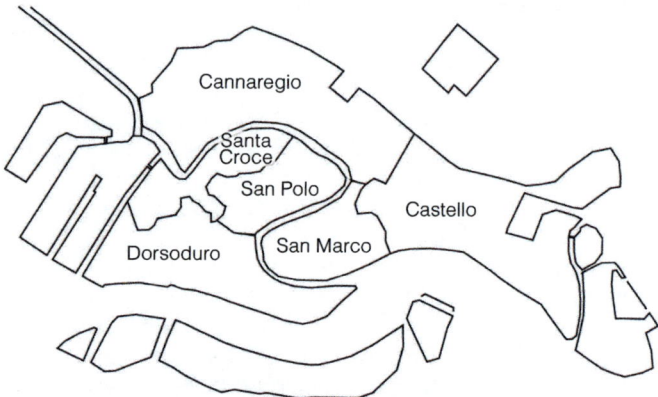

Group 5. Sestiere San Marco with Campo S. Vidal
Group 6. Sestiere Castello with Campo Santa Maria Formosa
Through a sequence of sketches in plan, section and small perspective vignettes, students presented their analysis describing their experience walking down the *insulae*. The urban survey of Venice included looking at the following:
1. Grid System: figure ground/orientation of main buildings in the selected *insula* in relation to the water system of the lagoon and *canal/rio* and the pedestrian system of *the fondamenta/riva/calli* including the north/south orientation
2. Threshold: analysing and representing the continuity/discontinuity and the edge conditions between the buildings in the selected insula analysing and representing the inside/outside relation of the selected building(s) with the open urban space (through plans and sections)
3. Materiality: architectural characteristics evident in the *insula* including specific materials / texture and colours if appropriate

Design proposals

Based on the analysis of the historical urban landscape of Venice, of the traditional configuration of the *insulae* and of the wide-open space of the *campos*, the students designed their first urban interpretation and proposals, looking at all of these components as tools to develop an organizing system of movement, urban activity and built environment. The students interpreted the project site of the Gas Area for an innovative and alternative scenario, proposing new land uses to react to the actual urban weaknesses and threats (for example the development of cultural activities) and using the traditional Venetian morphological tools with a new original interpretation (for example using the concept of visibility/invisibility of the built environment).

The narrative: site/context/brief critical exploration
Presenting a planning organization and a design strategy, the design teams demonstrated how the three components of architecture, landscape and interior were integrated in their preliminary design proposal. The new configuration is based on a critical interpretation of the urban/morphological analysis

Students analysis sketches

Comparison of old spaces and the project by architect G. Valle, students photos

of their selected insula and campo, the Gas Area project site analysis inserted in the specific context of Santa Marta and the understanding of its relation to Venice as a city.

Students were able to define an imaginative narrative for their urban configuration and the activities they wanted the users or visitors to experience integrating aspects of architectural, landscape and interior design intent. The narrative and the design themes were best condensed through the title of the six group projects: 1. Nexus, 2. Reclaiming Venice, 3. Impermanence, 4. Coalescence, 5. Treasure of Venice, 6. *Giardini* of the West.

By challenging **'movement'** with the design of the new light rail and station, **'activity'** with new residential and cultural activities and **'visibility'** with the new construction of landmark buildings and/or **invisibility** with the adaptation of the existing underused circular Gas Tanks, the six groups engaged with the problematic of the site and the vision for the future of this part of Venice, learning to appreciate it as a model for a modern city of the future.

Movement: access/circulation/exterior-interior spaces
All groups looked at the aspects of access to the site through public transportation of the new planned light rail system through water and land imagining a new configuration, which allowed movement through the site for pedestrians, bicycles in some specific parts of the site and water transportation. The mobility schemes designed in the different projects propose circulation from exterior urban places to the interior spaces of the existing and new architecture, creating an innovative inside/outside relationship.

Urban activity: site-context/architectural volume/exterior spaces/landscape

All groups responded with imagination to their developed narrative and chosen program with an architectural and landscape configuration, questioning how their projects would sit in their immediate context.
They explored the relationship of their design proposal to the other natural and manmade elements, buildings and landscape in the context and the new proposed open spaces, which were new *campos*, water basin, parks or other green spaces, etc. .

Student analysis, photos and sletches

Visibility/invisibility: transformation/adaptive reuse/preservation/built environment

The design development of the site might be also looked through the lens of visibility and invisibility. This concept comes from the reading of the transformation of the existing gas tanks, by focusing primarily on their interior adaptation and renovation thus maintaining their exterior built form, or demolishing them and adopting a new architecture to mark a specific urban activity within the site.
The interaction between the three systems of movement, urban activity and transformation or adaptation of the built environment (visibility/invisibility) was itself an interactive process that involved the students from initial simple design thoughts to more complex design interventions. Several proposals of adaptive reuses of the abandoned industrial buildings of the former gas factory were the most interesting result of this design process, creating a new integrated urban neighbourhood, where new building and old reused building worked together to create a contemporary new urban facade of the west part of Venice.

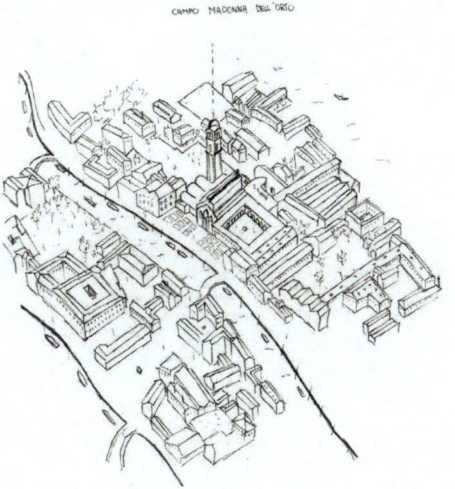

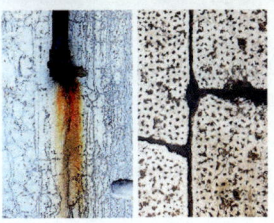

Nexus

1

Catriona Bisset

Shen Jia

Jackie Lee

Omer Mosman

Andrea Tommasin

Vanessa Wood

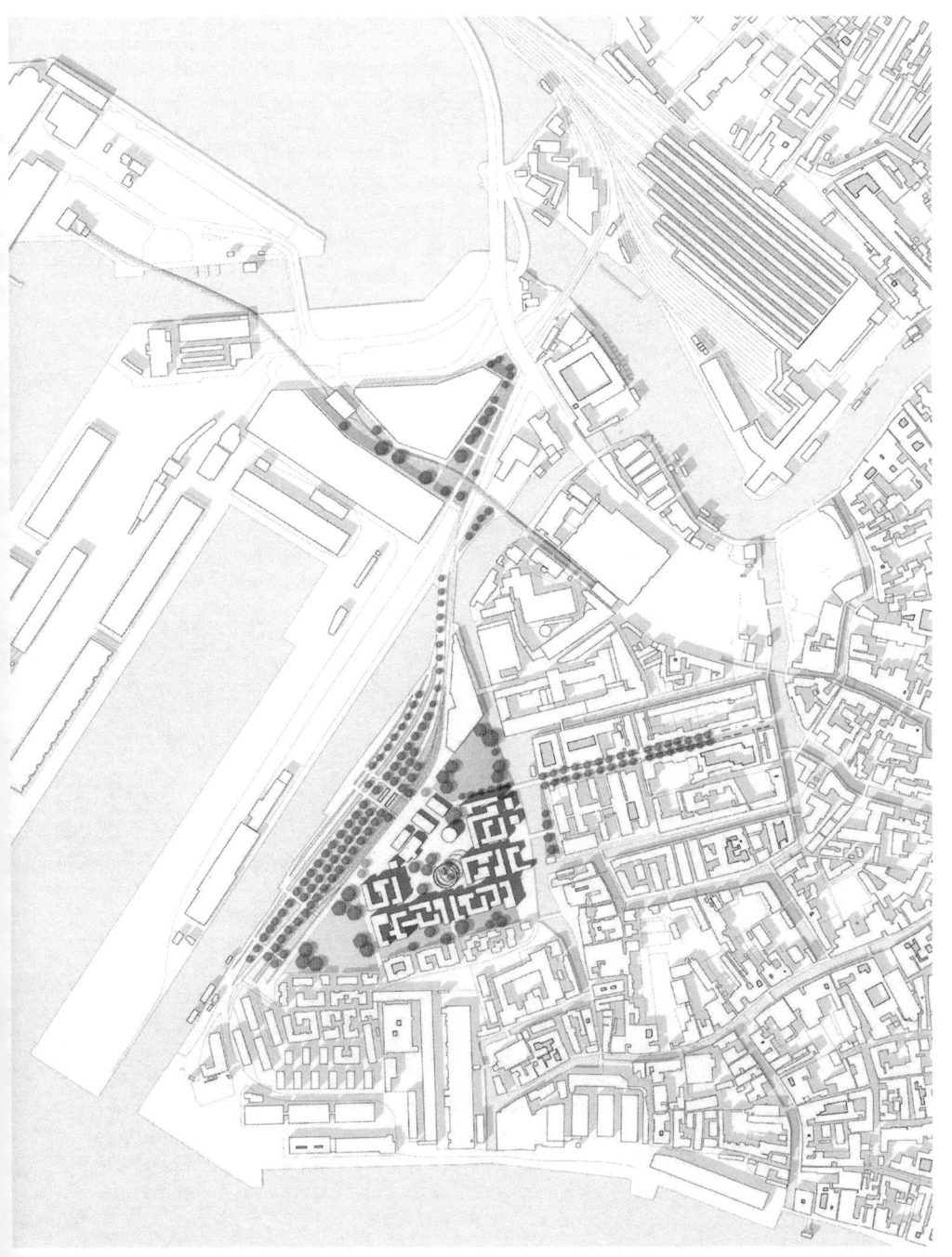

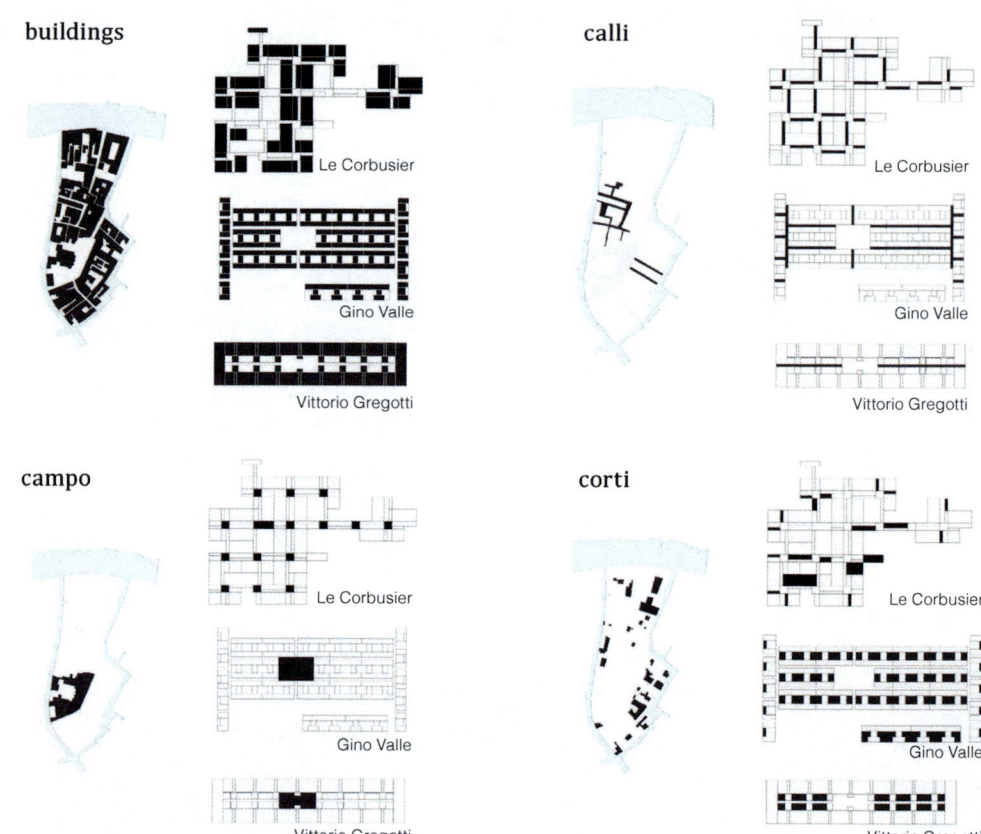

Analysis of the types of spaces in San Giacomo dell'Orio and in some venetian projects of Le Corbusier (1964), Gino Valle in Sacco Fisola (1980) and Vittorio Gregotti in San Giobbe (1984).

We conducted an analysis on Campo San Giacomo dell'Orio, from which the idea of 'Nexus' (that is a connection linking two or more things and also a central point) was generated.
The underlying concept of the space area of Campo San Giacomo dell'Orio consists of both compressed and decompressed spaces. From the analysis of the campo we observed the magnetic pull of the campo, being the heart of the space, and its ability to foster activity for both residents and visitors.
The compression and decompression formed a network of spaces that led to the central core, which contained a landmark. One of the main features of the campo was the community garden – bringing vegetation back to the Venetians and providing them with the opportunity to work together as a community.

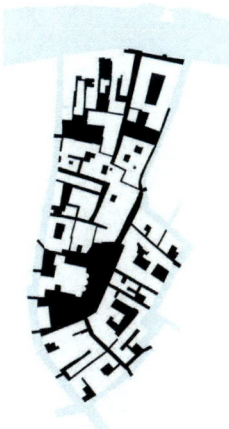
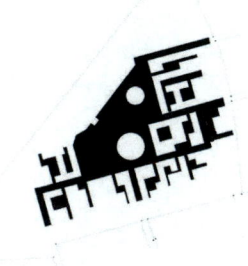

San Giacomo dell'Orio
voids

ex-Italgas

Compare of space typologies in San Giacomo dell'Orio and in the project area

bridges **campo** **calli** **secondary calli**

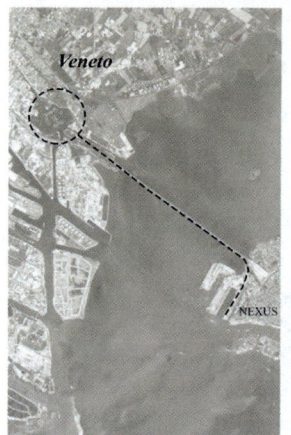

Location of the project diagram of the paths (tram, car, pedestrian) and design plan.

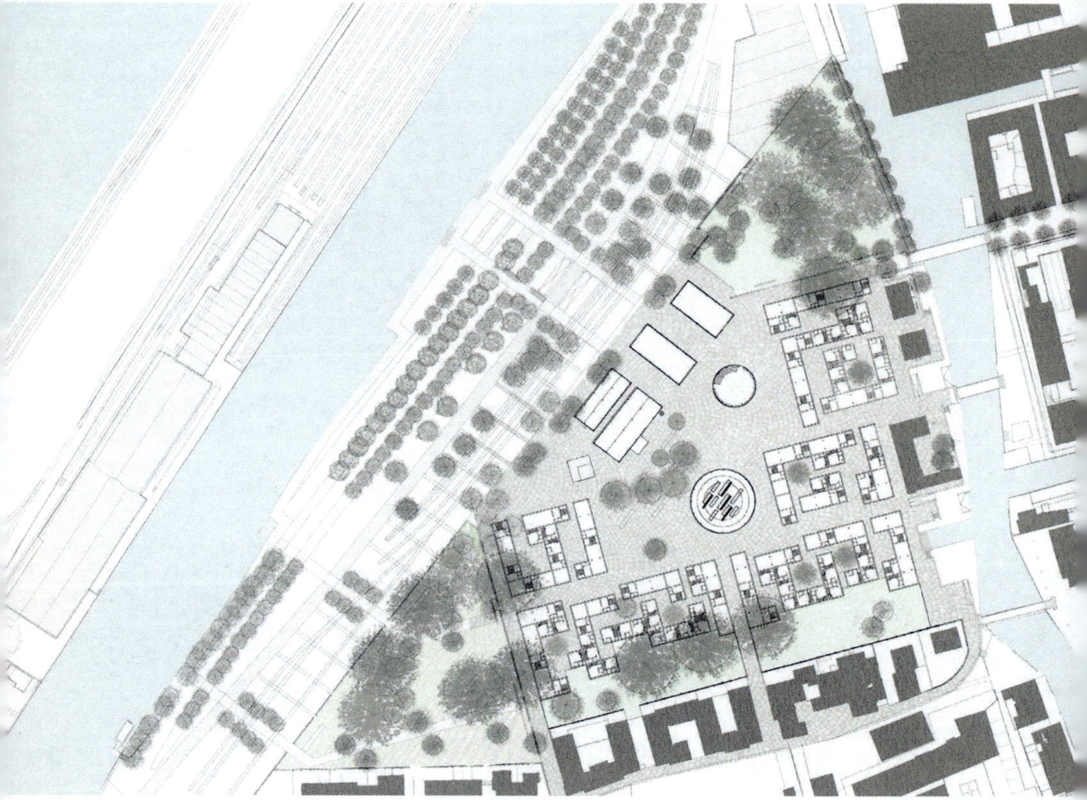

Nexus:
1. a connection linking two or more things
2. a central or focal point

Key concept:
1. compression/decompression
2. a network of spaces with a central heart
3. the community garden

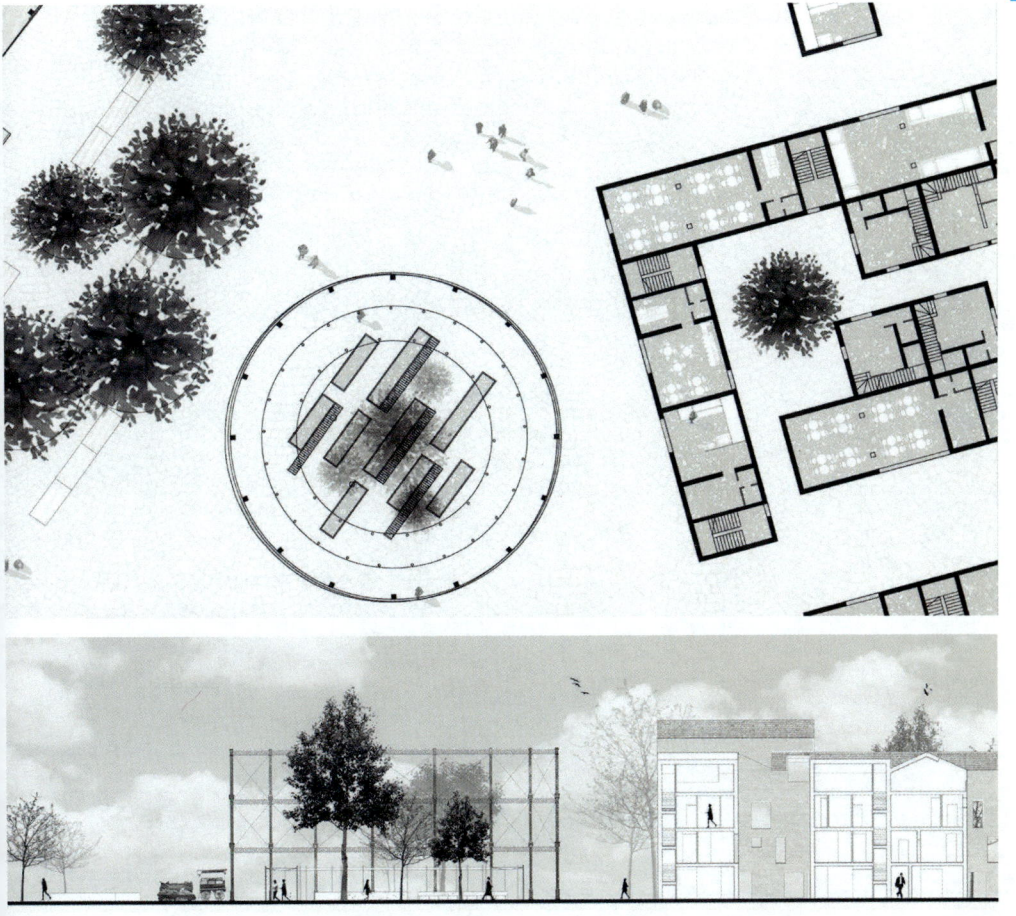

The Gasometer as a community garden in plan and section

The Nexus project aims to provide a contemporary take on the current Venetian urban system while maintaining the integral elements as derived from our campo study. It is a project about weaving people through a series of varying density of spaces, eventually pulling them into the open core. Agriculture is an activity we integrated into the site as a way of providing lush vegetation for the community, as well as to draw surrounding residents into the space. In this project we also aimed to provide a clear hierarchy of spaces and the filtering of public to private spaces.

We have chosen to retain the majority of the existing buildings and vegetation, including the existing gasometers which have been transformed into the landmarks of the new campo; one being an enclosed exhibition and auditorium space and the other being an open community garden.

Residential opportunities have been provided in the form of both houses and apartments both positioned in a more private sector of the site. The main access to the site is through a green belt that caters for pedestrians, bikes, cars and trams.

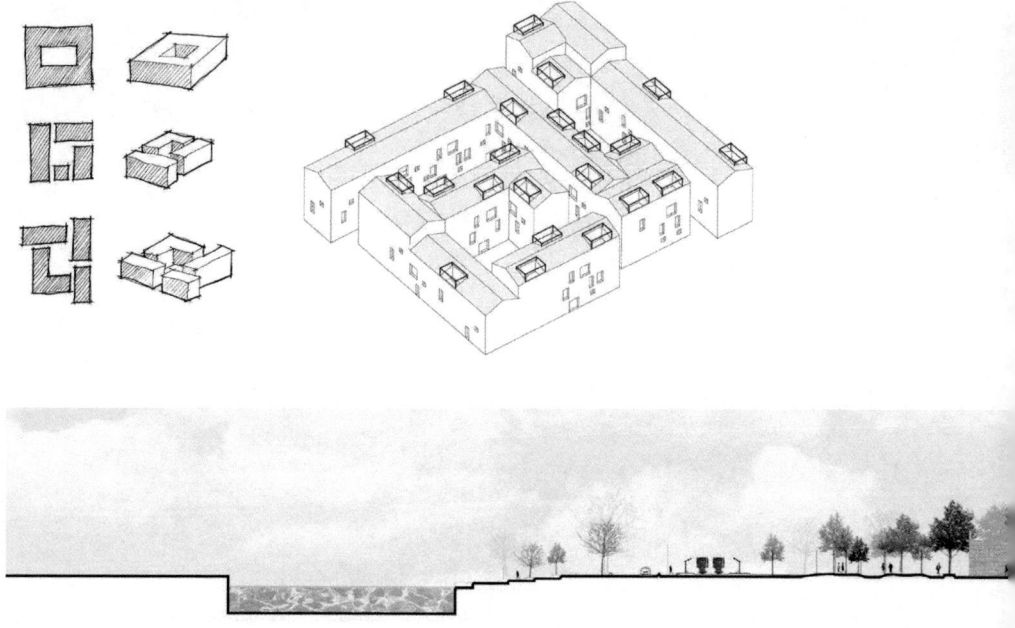

PREVIOUS PAGE:
residential building project and design process sketches. Section from west to east.

THIS PAGE:
existing gasometer transformed into an open community garden.

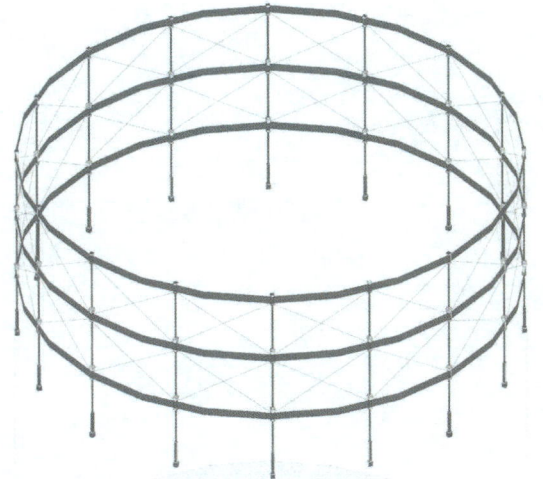

steel structure

canvas shading

produce market

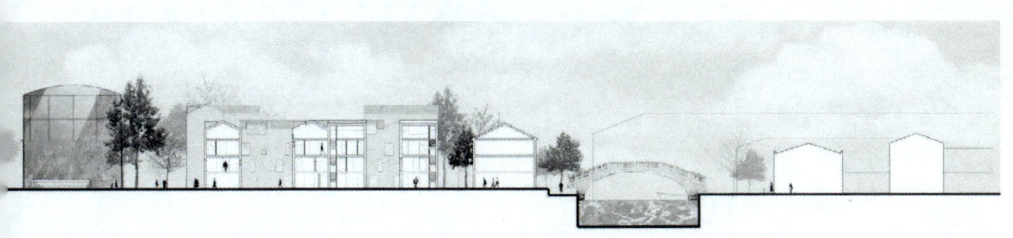

Reclaiming Venice

2

Mingmin Liu

Aurelie

Nadia Hendryani

Julia Lau

Simone Rego

Analysis of existing services in Venice:

- ■ public green areas
- ■ not accessible green areas
- ■ gym
- ■ football fields
- ■ rowing schools
- ■ swimming pools
- ■ tennis fields
- ■ cinema
- ■ theatre

- ■ exibition spaces
- ■ residential facilities projects
- ■ decaying buildings

Project area: circulation, sport facilities and other amenities location (exibition, performance spaces, restaurant, bar, market, artisans spaces)

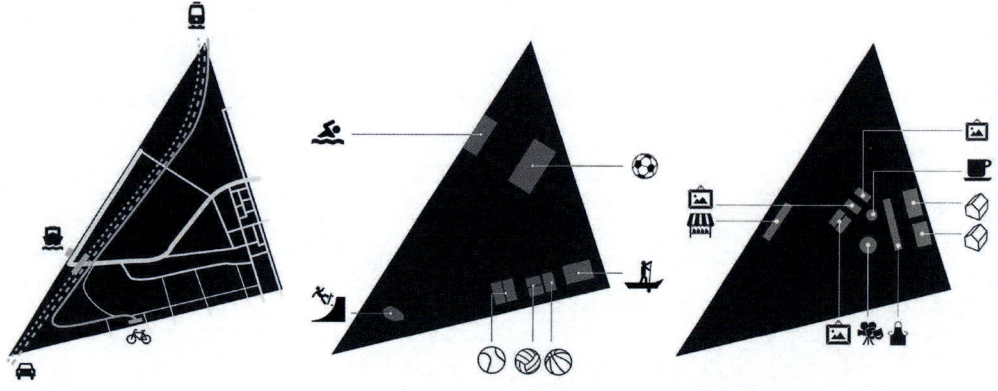

The city of Venice is abundant in historical significance and rich in culture. However, due to the movement of business and consequently of residents toward the mainland and the increase in tourism, Venice's culture and the remaining residents' lifestyle have been dulled by a city overrun by tourists.

Our project aims to introduce facilities that will cater for the existing residential area and the new developments currently in progress in other sites, such as the student housing to the south of the area, and the new residential buildings on la Giudecca.

With many buildings already falling to decay as the residential population decreases, we propose that the majority of the design should be a public, community space that focuses on services for the existing residents and to provide Venetians with experiences that are lacking in their city, rather than new residential developments.

The project emphasis is on the campo as vital centre for artisans and craftsmen of Venice, thus celebrating Venice as a vessel for artistic expression.

The existing industrial buildings are transformed into exhibition, performance spaces and a restaurant and bar.

These elements create the main hub of the site and cater not only for the artisans, but also for the students of the art and architecture schools.

Surrounding the campo are sports facilities such as a football pitch, indoor and outdoor swimming pools, biking facilities, embedded in a large, undulating expanse of green space that forms its own individual spaces.

A series of community gardens border the site with a small collection of residential buildings based upon the existing buildings already on the site.

Sketch of the project area

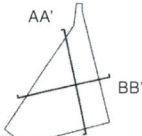

Transverse and longitudinal sections of the project area. Design model.

AA'

BB'

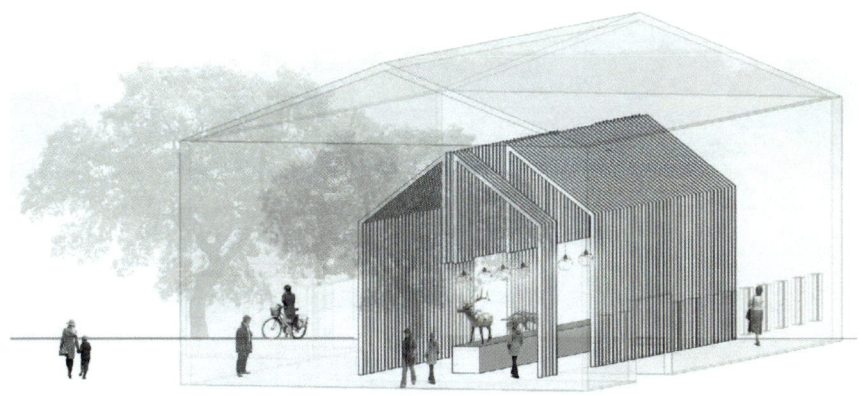

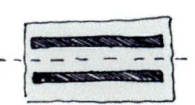   

Exhibition space in an existing building, axonometric view and diagrams. Below, section of the renovated gasometer.

Exploded drawing of the design elements on one of the twin buildings

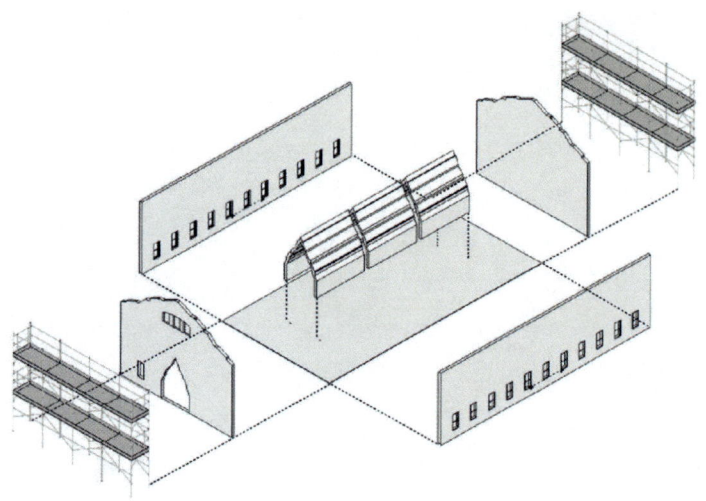

The pictures on these pages show the architectural intervention on the existing buildings. By inserting a number of freestanding internal wood structures without touching the old walls, the project transforms them into exhibition spaces.

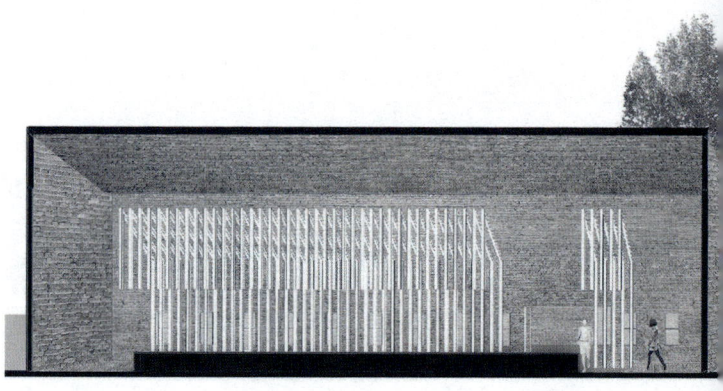

Section and diagrams of one of the
twin buildings

 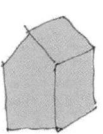  

Imper manence

3 Amber Gallen
Enrica Pavan
Francesco Orteschi
Johnny Ellice-Flint
Jun Loh

Impermanence as a central design notion came from an in-depth investigation and analysis of the Campo Della Pescheria, a Venetian square in the San Polo sestiere. The campo functions in almost complete perpetuity, as a fresh food and fish market from early morning to early afternoon. Though the campo is physically located directly on the Canal Grande, the activity and focus of the urban space is completely introspective and impermanent.

The concept of impermanence was applied to the allocated project site on Santa Marta as an approach to create a new Sestiere of Venice with flexibility and diversity that is not found anywhere else on the island.
This driving force has been pulled through the entire site with the Western edge of the new sestiere articulated as an interpretation of the mudflats and ecologically rich tidal zones found throughout the Venetian lagoon, that could interact directly with the urban fabric of Venice. This edge is never set or defined, but rather completely dependent on the tides, sediment movement and gradual plant migration - structured loosely around a grid of vertical timber pylons that are informed by the existing railways on the site. The aim was also to create a development that would become a precedent for the reintroduction of natural systems and ecological impermanence into the main islands of Venice.

Tramline

Diagram with the new position of the tramline and the main elements that define the masterplan.

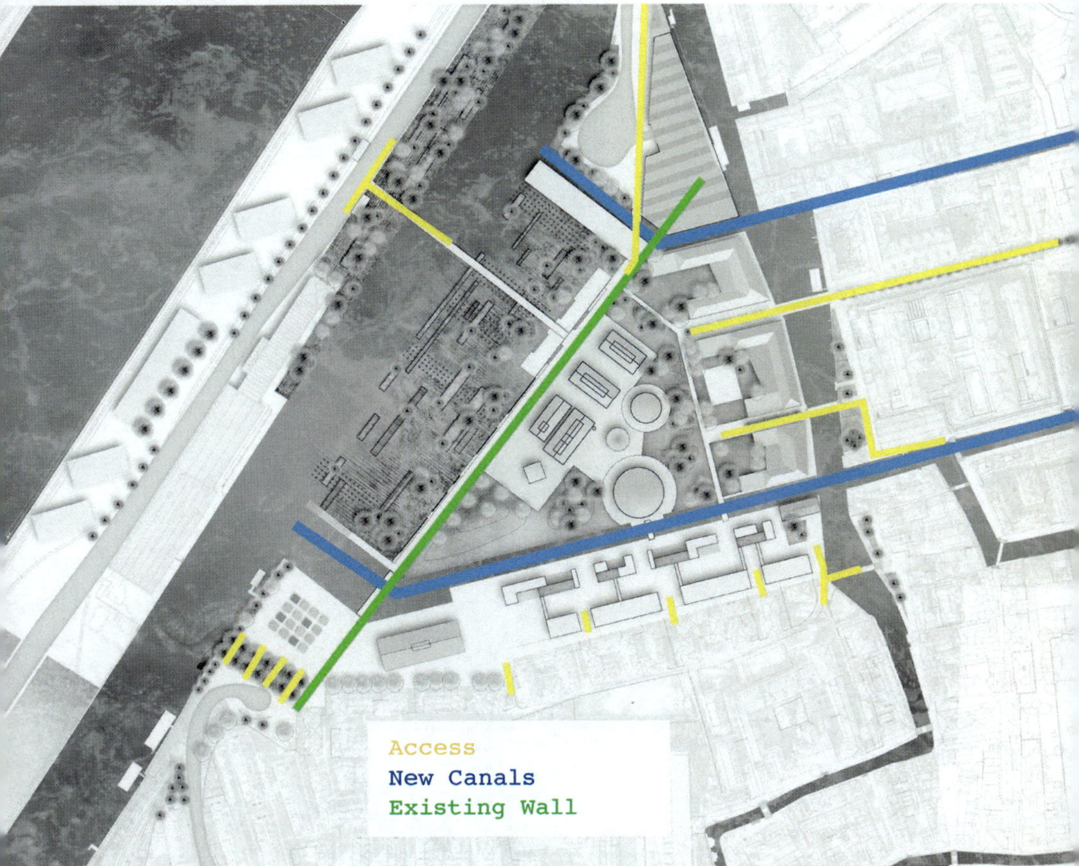

Access
New Canals
Existing Wall

Diagram during high tidal (above) and low tidal (below)

Sections of the wetlands along the west shore of the project area

The architectural spaces and forms have been carefully considered in regards to the diversity of space and usage whilst being sensitive to the existing cultural surroundings and residences. The cultural hub is focused on the gentle complexities of the human senses and their relationship to impermanence. The notion that what we see, feel and touch are all passing experiences that we cannot hold onto was a driving force behind designing.

Sections project of one of the twin buildings

Bell tower, plan, section, elevation
and simulation view of the interior.

Section and simulation view of the gasometer

Coale scence

4

Parise Chyssargis

Lisa Cohen

Jonathan Yip

Meidan Yin

Lubna Matar

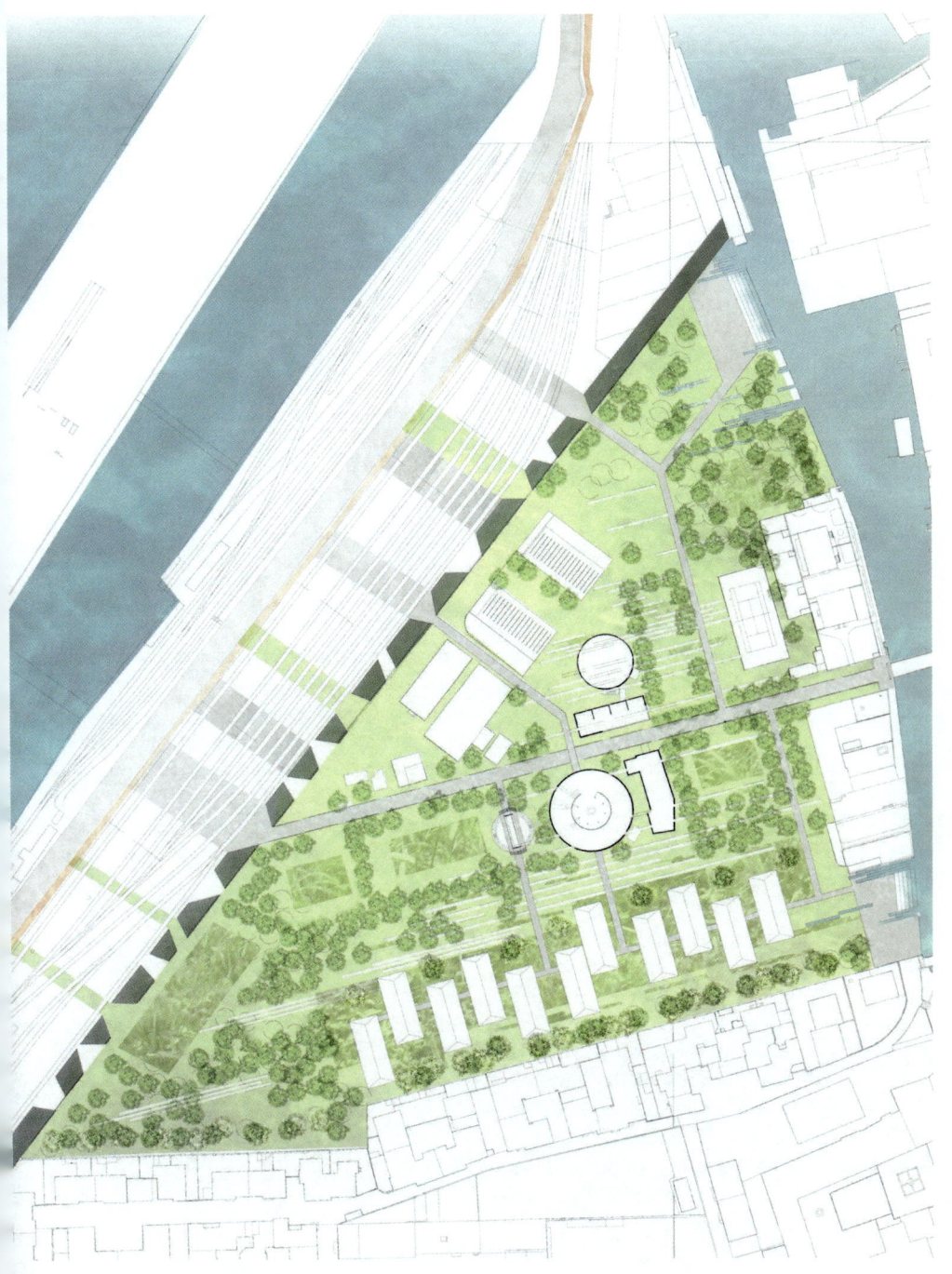

Map of Venice created by the number of geotagged photos uploaded on Flickr and Picasa search APIs. Source: Eric Fischer
https://www.flickr.com/photos/walkingsf/

Inspired by our analysis of Campo Madonna Dell' Orto, our design explores a sense of ambiguity and continuity through the spaces, providing Venetians with a refuge from the city centre and tourist areas. After an analysis of Eric Fisher's diagrammatic street map referencing main tourist routes in Venice, it became clear that a place to 'escape' was necessary to enrich the quality of lives of the residents in the area.

In light of this, we see our site as a cultural hub. Our design incorporates a multitude of facilities and provides opportunities for the residents to enjoy a sense of comfort and intimacy within the many spaces.

By allowing the existing landscape to guide our design strategy, we emphasise both the material transitions and the architectural spaces, as blurred elements to exploit the boundaries.

Thus a sense of fluidity is introduced in our design as one form morphs into another, highlighting concepts of continuity and transience.

The interplay between exterior and interior helps to facilitate this fluid notion - an element inspired by the site visit in Cannaregio.

In an attempt to use traditional elements of architecture in a non-conventional way, the language of an arched colonnade is repeated through the scheme (another element derived from the architecture at Campo Madonna Dell'Orto).

Overall, through a strong integration between landscape and urban architecture, a sense of coherence is established, providing a peaceful and comfortable escape for those who experience it.

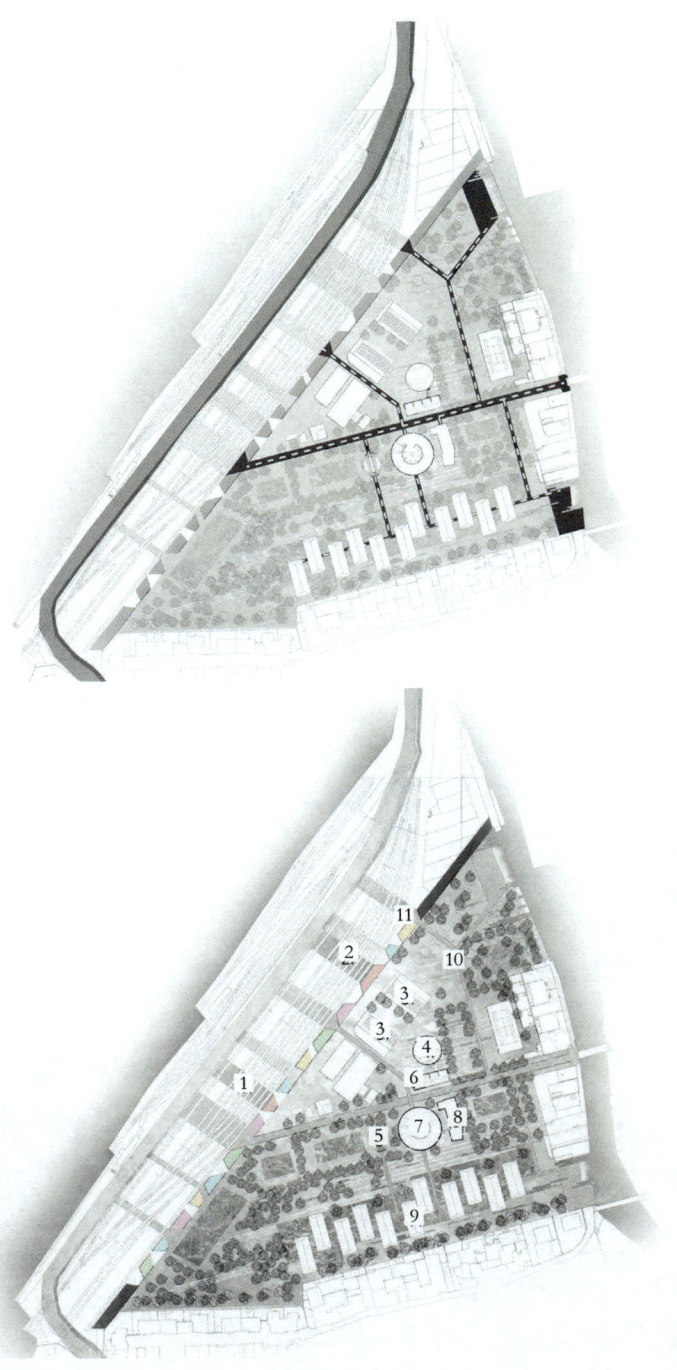

Circulation diagram

Functions:
1. market area
2. tram stop and shelter
3. garden I
4. garden II
5. cafe I
6. cafe II
7. library / cultural hub
8. music / dance studio
9. residential
10. water feature
11. wall

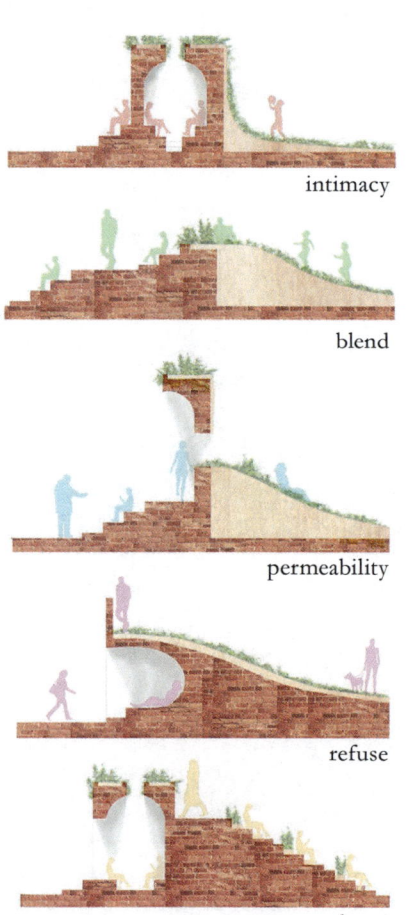

intimacy

blend

permeability

refuse

learn

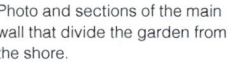

Photo and sections of the main wall that divide the garden from the shore.

Section of the library and interior view of the garden inside one of the twin building.

Some study sketches of the wall and a section.

Below, east-west and north-south sections.

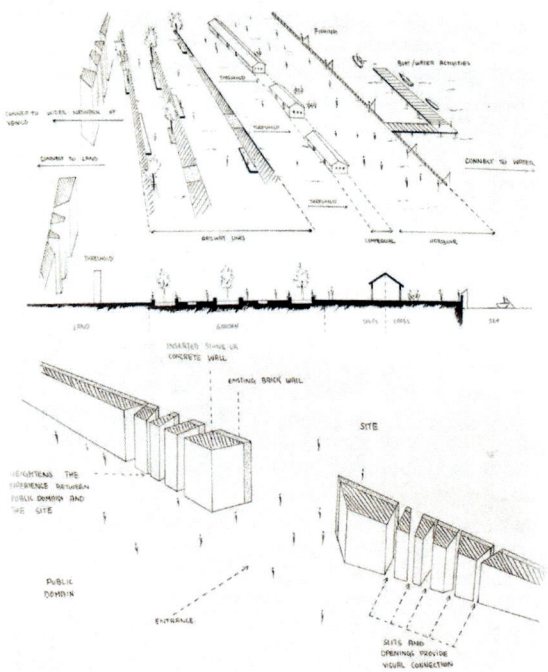

Coalescence:
1. to grow together;
2. to unite in a whole : fuse

A place for refuge:
1. shelter, protection from;
2. escape

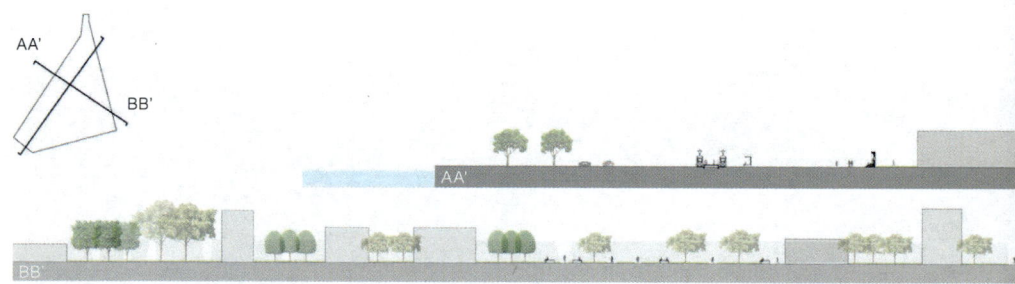

View of the garden with water feature

Below, plan of the southern boundary of the area with the project and the existing residential buildings.

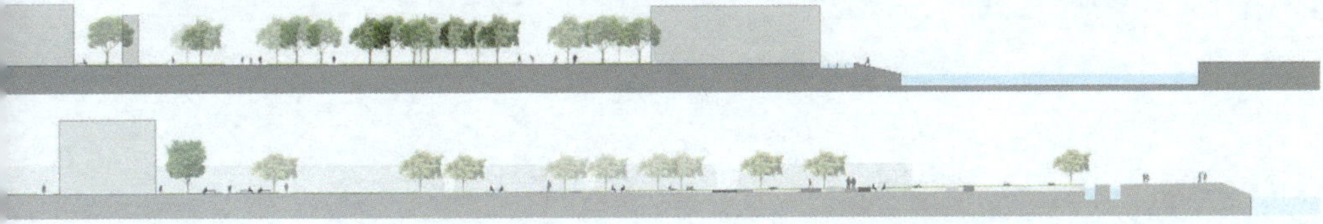

Treasure of Venice

5

Allison Sainty

Ashleigh Bennett

Marco Carraro

Niloofar Meshgini

Tommaso Gomiero

Yvonne Chan

Rawail Khan

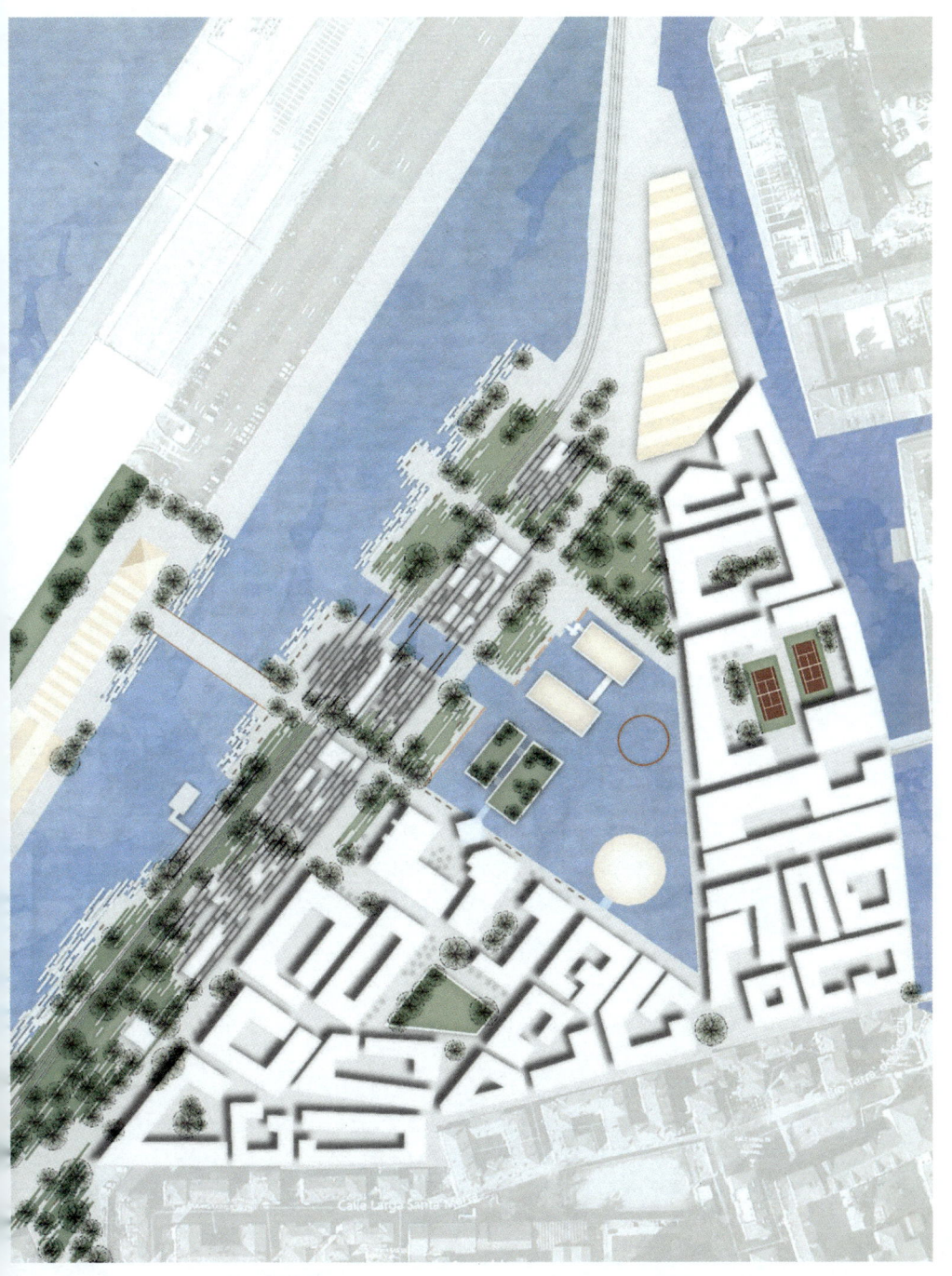

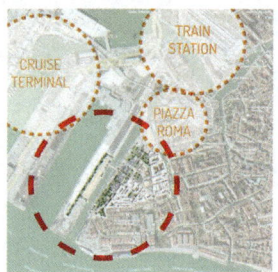

Venice has had a symbiotic relationship with the water surrounding it since it was first conceived as a settlement centuries ago. Through our design development, we have played with this idea of water, structuring the site around a newly constructed canal and flooded public zone. This flooded area allowed us to having several existing structures floating as sculptures celebrating the relationship between Venice and the water.
A public library, cafe, art gallery, exhibition spaces and theatre now occupy the existing structures of the former Italgas site.

This idea of floating, or hovering above the water, has continued throughout the site, with various planes floating above, around and below, from a shade structure reminiscent of the old rail yards in the public waterfront, to moveable hovering facades along the retail frontages, right through to the interior details of the public library. Our analysis of Campo San Vidal reinforced the idea of Venice's tradition of small bridges and walkways.

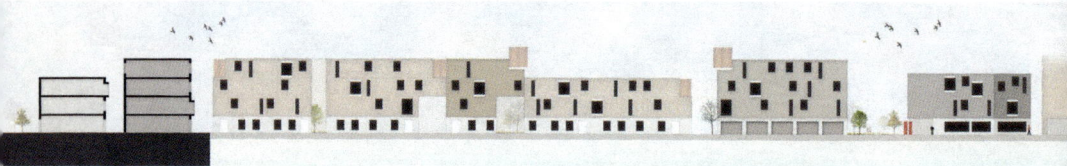

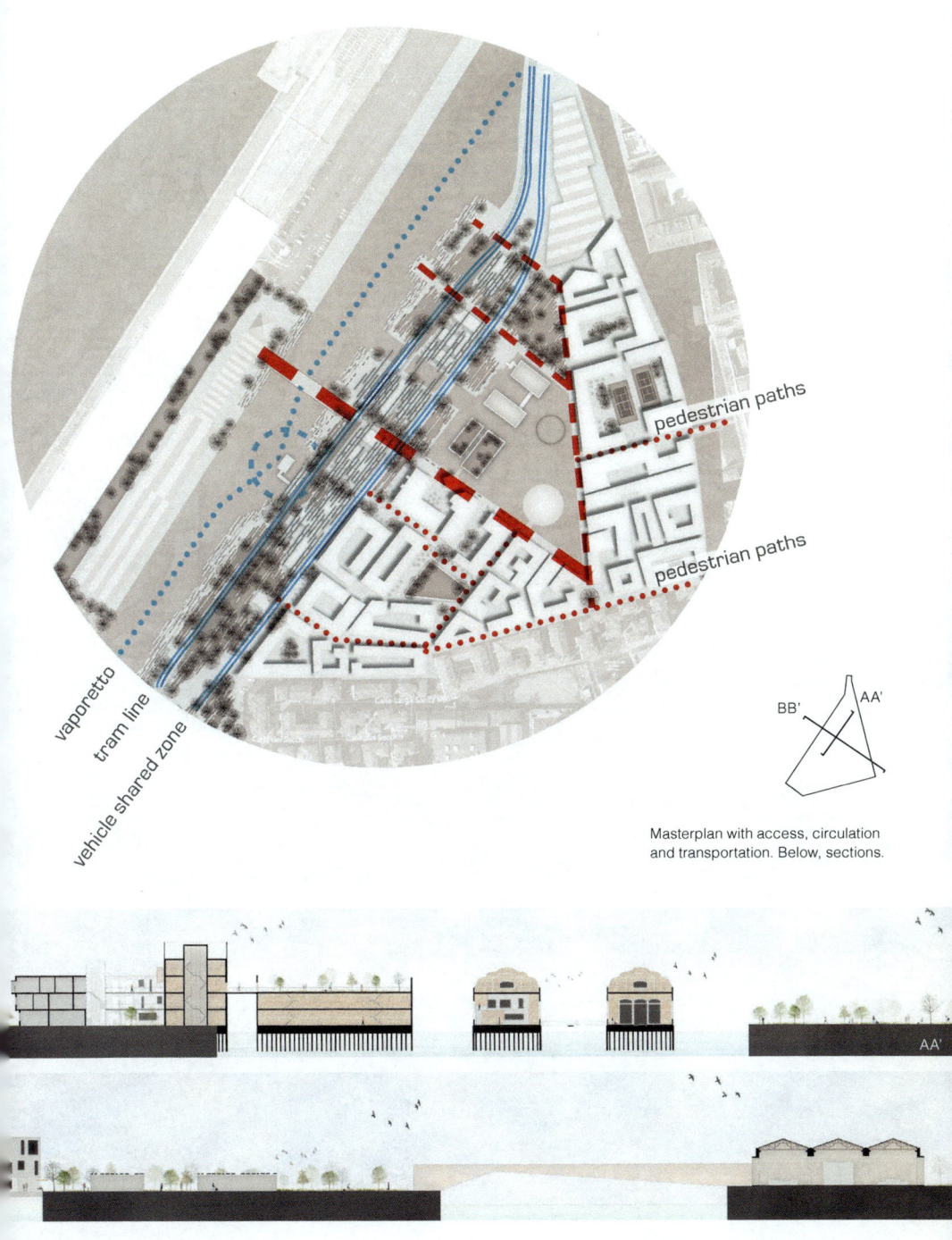

Masterplan with access, circulation and transportation. Below, sections.

Draft masterplan:

- accesses to the area (PINK CIRCLES)
- transport lines (PINK and PURPLE DOTTED LINES)
- waterfront (area circled with a GREEN DOTTED LINE)
- market space (area circled with a RED DOTTED LINE)
- functions (indicated by WHITE ARROWS)
- project references (circles on sides)

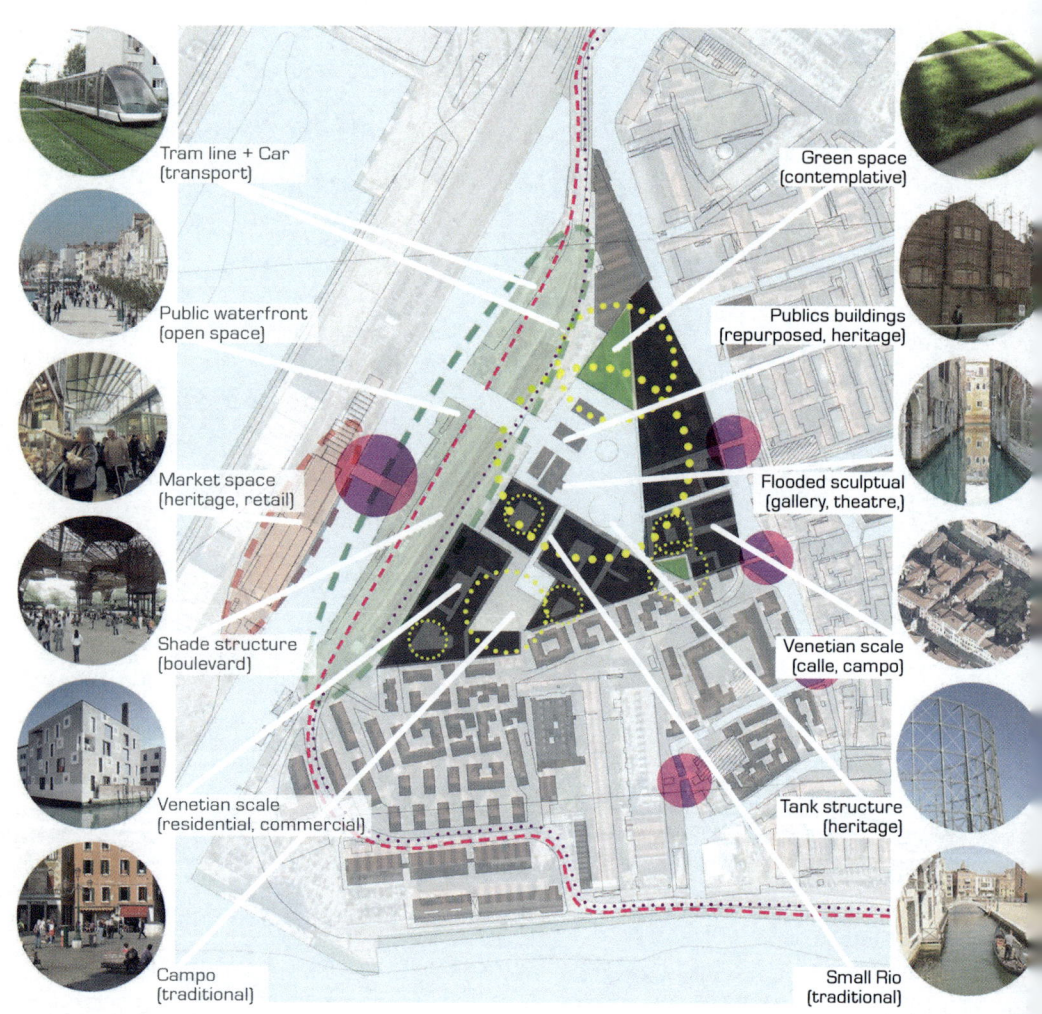

Simulations of some views on the waterfront and the new water basin inside the ex-Italgas area.

Sketches and view of the new water bassin.

This led us to design a mixed use and residential area by creating small passageways and courtyards to provide a true Venetian experience. That experience of winding through built forms, apparently lost in the circulation system yet cleverly leading you towards the public spaces. It is this true experience of Venice we wanted to retain.

Our concept for the Italgas site invites you to explore, search out and find a true treasure of Venice - the new cultural hub and open waterfront, a true treasure in the compact urban form of this old city.

Simulation views and plants of the existing twin buildings transformed into a public library and cafe.

Ground floor   First floor

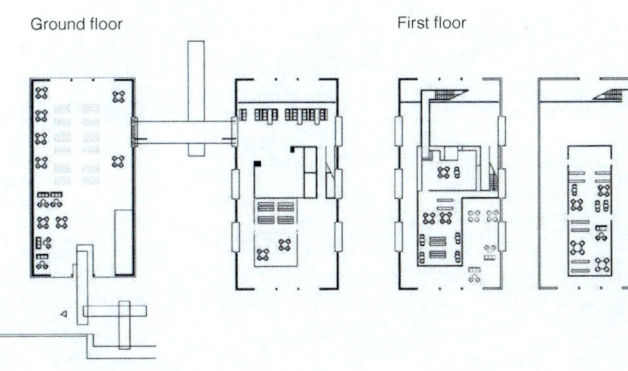

Giardini of the West

6

Annie Tran

Dean Kim

Fabio Matteazzi

Jessica Li

Maria Imbrigliati

Rawail Khan

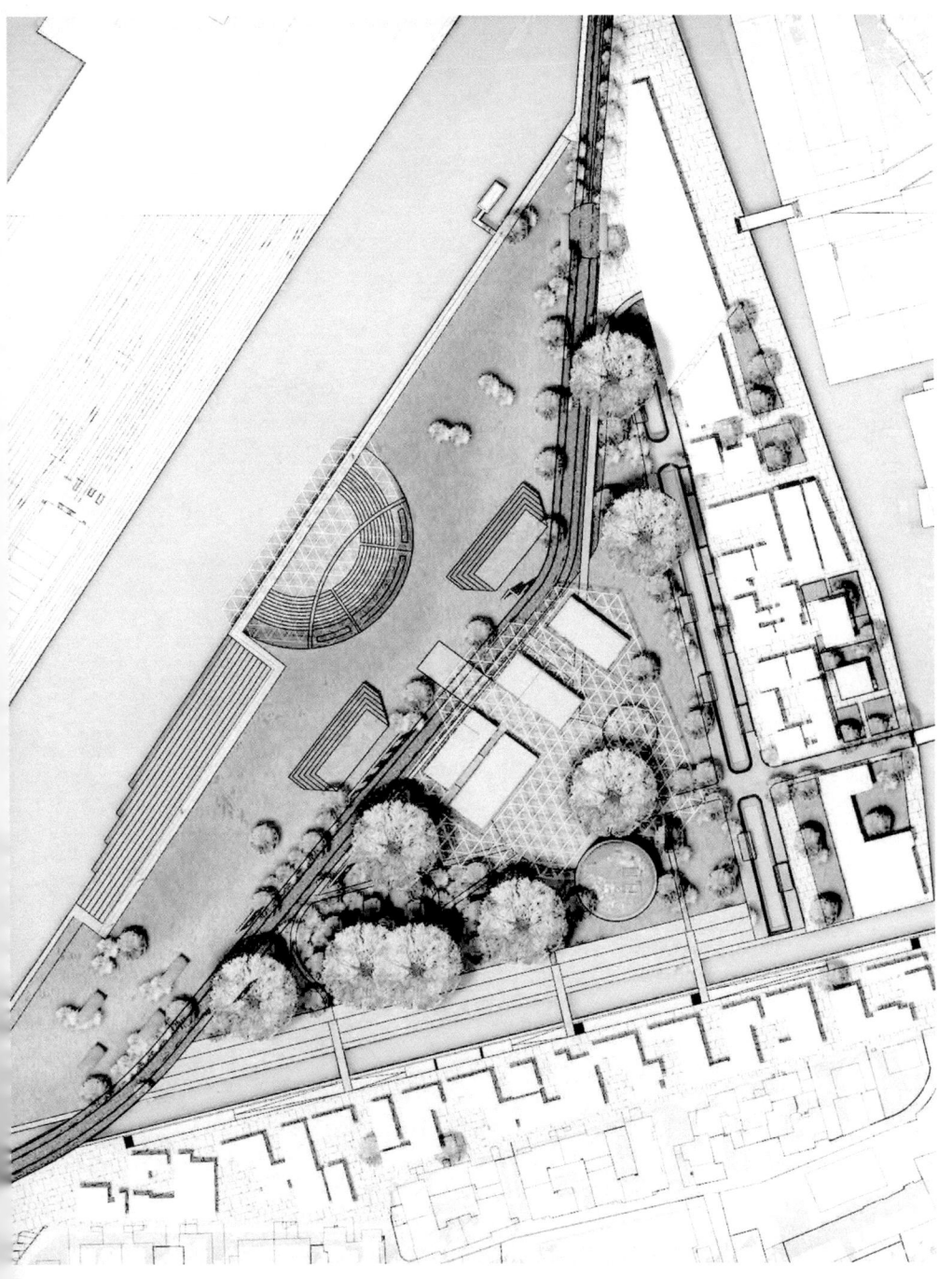

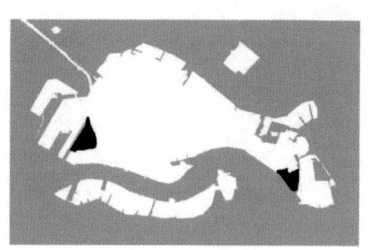

Giardini of the West explores the possibility of introducing a cultural hub that celebrates a form of art separate to the global architecture that is celebrated at the Biennale.
More specifically, this project celebrates dance and music production.

The location of the assigned site is on the western and more recently developed side of Venice.

The project is based on the analysis of the surrounding context and the greater Venice area, which encompassed investigating locations of nearby canals and landmarks, the transport systems, the universities' location and the Biennale Giardini activities situated on the opposite end of the island.
This opened further paths of research into the functions, aesthetics, organisation, limitations and advantages of the current Biennale and how it could influence the design of the proposed Giardini of the West.

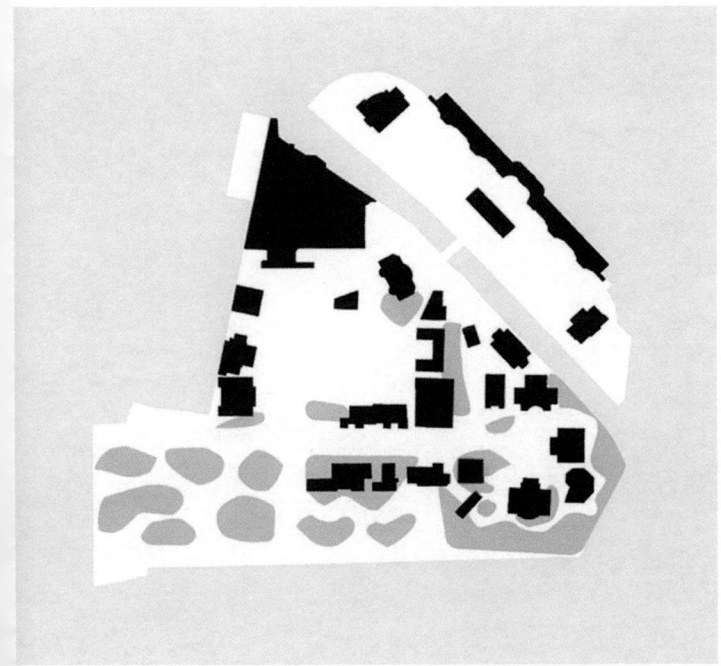

Venice scheme highlighting the ex-italgas area and the Giradini. Compare drawings between the gardens of the project area (left) and the gardens headquarters of the Bienniale (right)

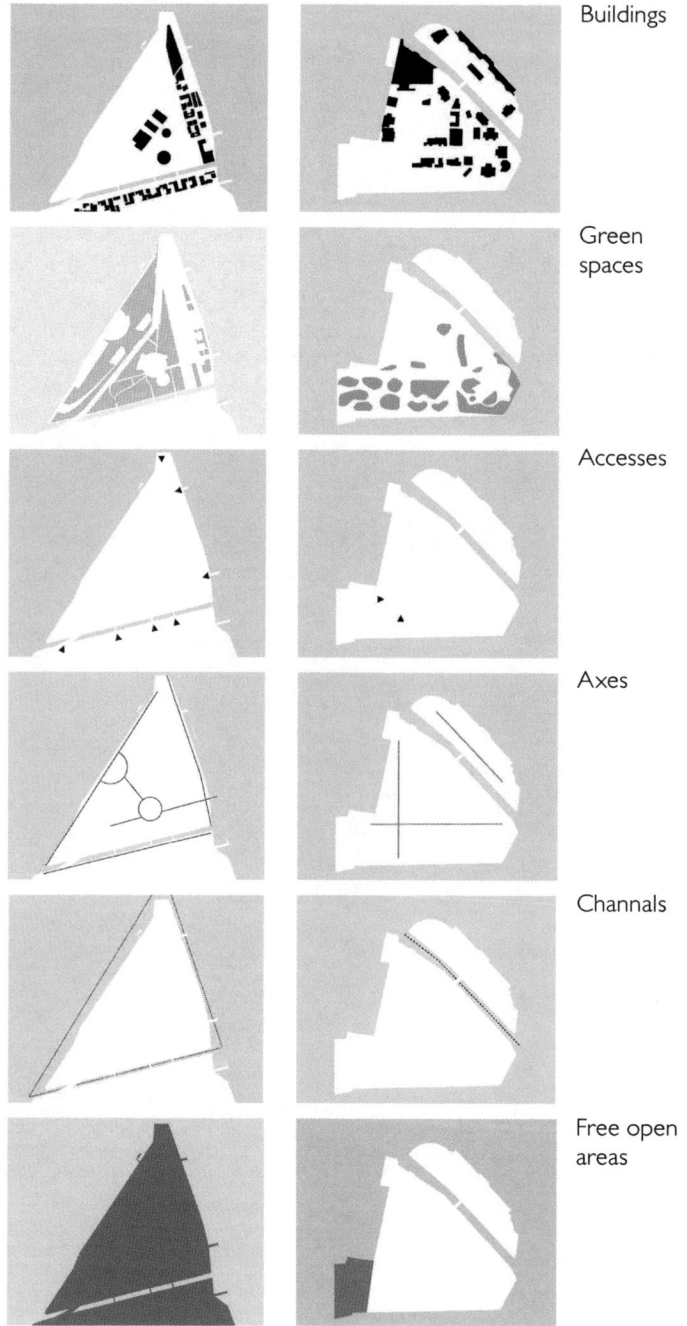

Parallel between the gardens of the project area (left) and the gardens headquarters of the Bienniale (right)

The aim was to utilize the model of the existing Biennale Giardini and create a more modern and improved Giardini which offered something different and in a better manner.

The main tool used to drive the planning organization and the design of the overall scheme, was the idea of contrast.
The proposed Giardini and the existing one contrastingly sit in opposite geographical locations within Venice.
This tool was used to explore contrasting characteristics of design.

While the buildings in the Biennale Giardini are scattered across the landscape, in the new Giardini of the West two central pathways define the circulation of the area and consequently the form and design of its landscape, the organisation of the residential strip and the cultural hub.

Masterplan with the functions of the cultural hub

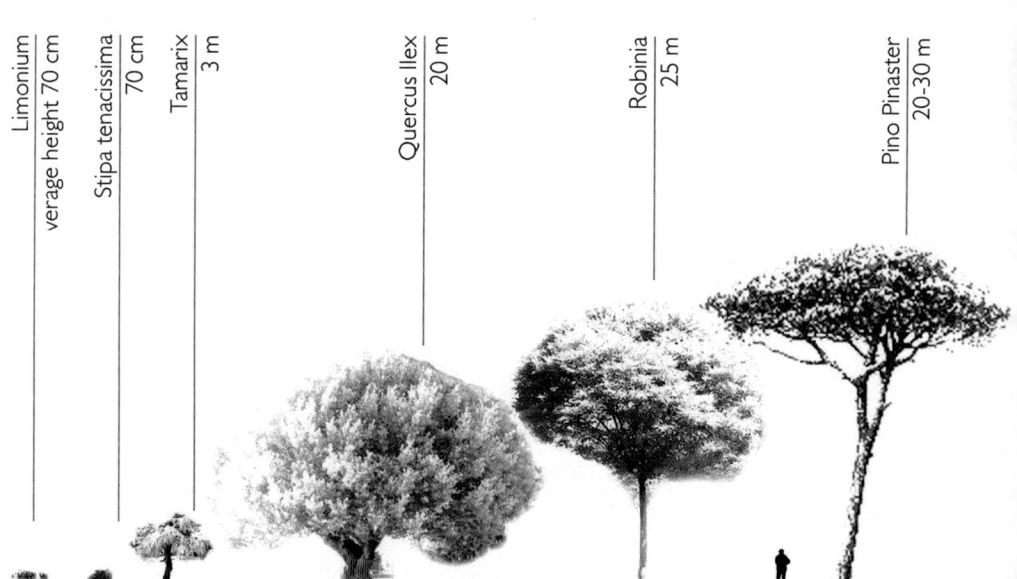

Trees project schedule in plant and section.

Relationship with the water:

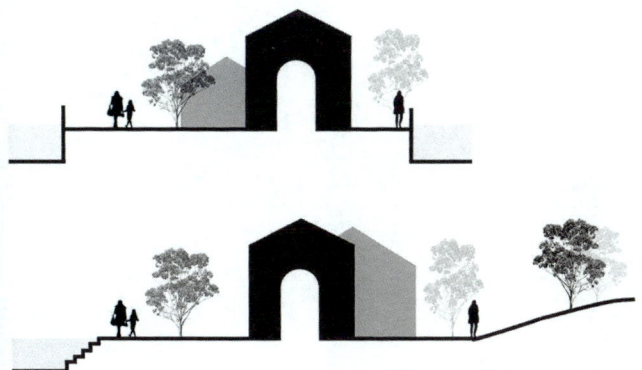

Giardini biennale

Giardini ex-Italgas

Perspective view of the interactive water feature.

The International Venice Studio is a Workshop held by the University IUAV of Venice and the University of New South Wales (UNSW) of Sydney at Palazzo Badoer in Venice from November 24th to December 5th, 2014.

Professors
Enrico Fontanari (IUAV)
Paola Favaro (UNSW)
Katrina Simon (UNSW)

Tutor
Anna-Paola Pola (IUAV)

Students
Catriona Bisset, Ashleigh Bennett, Marco Carraro, Yvonne Chan, Parise Chyssargis, Lisa Cohen, Marco de Stavola, John Ellice-Flint, Micol Galeotti, Amber Gallen, Tommaso Gomiero, Nadia Hendryani, Maria Imbrigliati, Shen Jia, Rawail Khan, Dean Kim, Julia Lau, Jackie Lee, Jessica Li, Mingmin Liu, Jun Loh, Lubna Matar, Fabio Matteazzi, Niloofar Meshgini, Omer Mosman, Aurelie Nguyen, Francesco Orteschi, Enrica Pavan, Simone Rego, Allison Sainty, Annie Tran, Andrea Tommasin, Vanessa Wood, Meidan Yin, Jonathan Yip

| I U A V | Università Iuav di Venezia | DIPARTIMENTO DI CULTURE DEL PROGETTO

LAUREA MAGISTRALE IN ARCHITETTURA E CULTURE DEL PROGETTO | DIPARTIMENTO DI ARCHITETTURA COSTRUZIONE CONSERVAZIONE

LAUREA MAGISTRALE IN ARCHITETTURA PER IL NUOVO E L'ANTICO | UNIVERSITY OF NEW SOUTH WALES - UNSW SIDNEY |

VENICE GATEWAY

workshop

24.11>5.12.2014
Badoer
San Polo 2468
Venezia

Progetti urbani e paesaggistici per la riqualificazione del fronte ovest di Venezia
Enrico Fontanari, Iuav
Paola Favaro, UNSW

aperto agli iscritti alla magistrale in architettura di DCP e DACC - **4 crediti tipologia D**
info e iscrizioni: henry@iuav.it - www.iuav.it

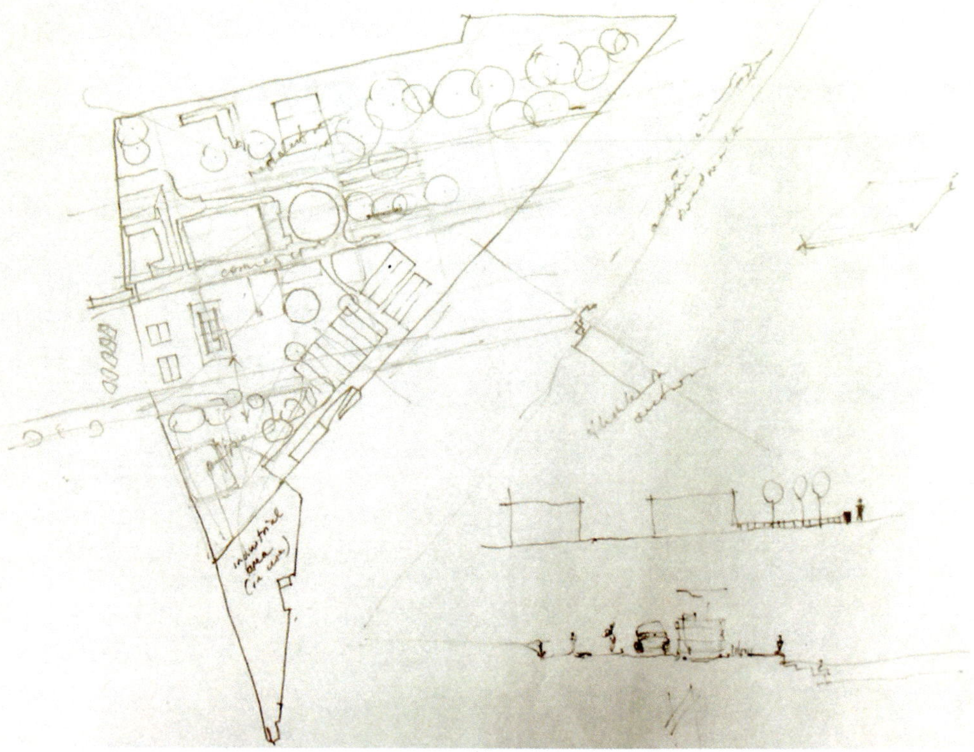

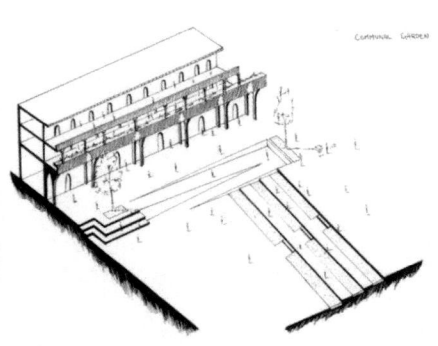

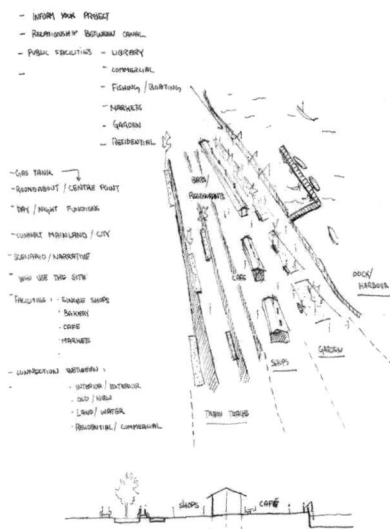

HIERARCHY OF OPENINGS : LAND

HIERARCHY OF OPENINGS : WATER

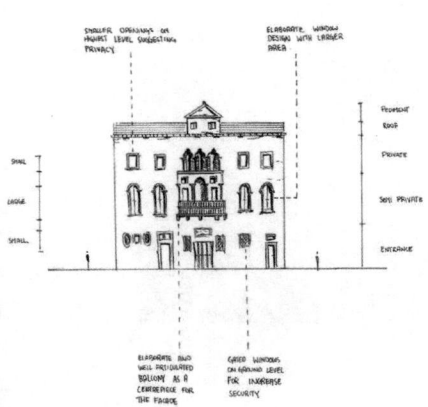

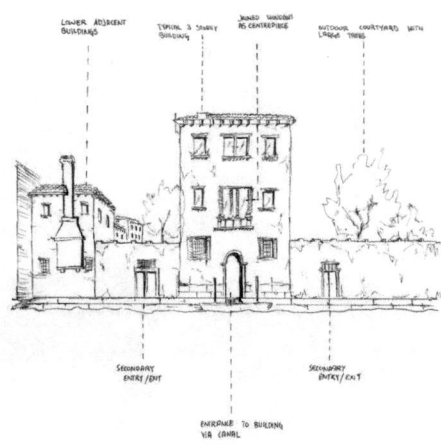

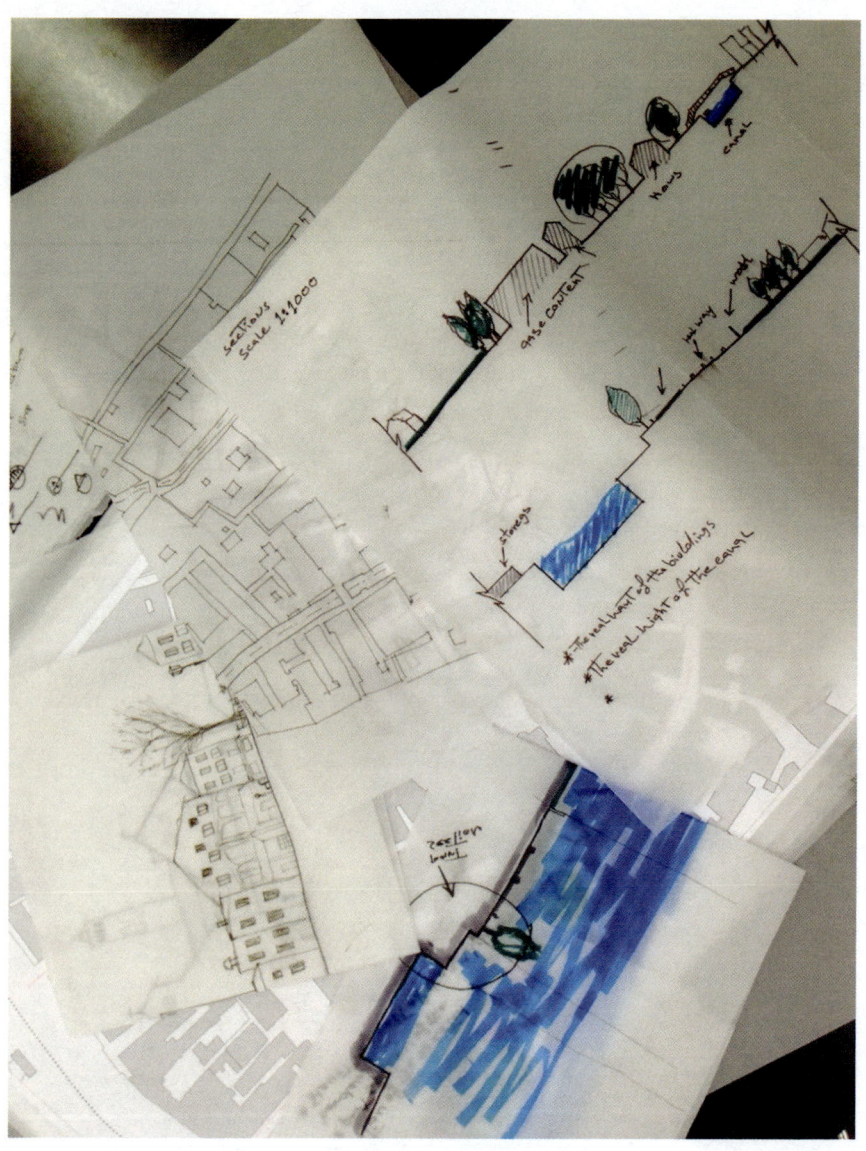

a New Gateway for Venice

Pubblicato da
LISt Lab
info@listlab.eu
listlab.eu

Produzione
GreenTrenDesign Factory
Piazza Manifattura, 1
38068 Rovereto (TN) - Italy
T: +39 0464 443427
info@greentrendesign.it

Edited by Paola Favaro,
Anna-Paola Pola and Katrina Simon

Direttore Editoriale
Pino Scaglione

Graphic coordination
Anna-Paola Pola

Assistente Editoriale
Gioia Marana

Art Director & Graphic Design
Blacklist Creative Studio, Barcelona
blacklist-creative.com

ISBN 9788898774647

Stampato e rilegato in Unione Europea,
Gennaio 2016

Tutti i diritti riservati
© dell'edizione LISt Lab
© dei testi gli autori
© delle immagini

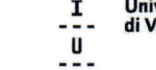

Promozione e distribuzione in Italia
Messaggerie Libri, Spa, Milano,
Numero verde 800.804.900
assistenza.ordini@meli.it;
fax 02.84406056;
amministrazione.vendite@meli.it
fax 02.84406057

Promozione e distribuzione internazionale
ActarD, USA
ACC, London

Comitato Scientifico delle edizioni List
Eve Blau (Harvard GSD), Maurizio Carta (Università di Palermo), Eva Castro (Architectural Association London) Alberto Clementi (Università di Chieti), Alberto Cecchetto (Università di Venezia), Stefano De Martino (Università di Innsbruck), Corrado Diamantini (Università di Trento), Antonio De Rossi (Università di Torino), Franco Farinelli (Università di Bologna), Carlo Gasparrini (Università di Napoli), Manuel Gausa (Università di Genova), Giovanni Maciocco (Università di Sassari/Alghero), Antonio Paris (Università di Roma), Mosè Ricci (Università di Genova), Roger Riewe (Università di Graz), Pino Scaglione (Università di Trento).

LISt Lab è un Laboratorio editoriale, con sedi in Europa, che lavora intorno ai temi della contemporaneità. LISt Lab ricerca, propone, elabora, promuove, produce, LISt Lab mette in rete e non solo pubblica.

LISt Lab editoriale è una società sensibile ai temi del rispetto ambientale-ecologico. Le carte, gli inchiostri, le colle, le lavorazioni in genere, sono il più possibile derivanti da filiere corte e attente al contenimento dell'inquinamento. Le tirature dei libri e riviste sono costruite sul giusto consumo di mercato, senza sprechi ed esuberi da macero. LISt Lab tende in tal senso alla responsabilizzazione di autori e mercato e ad una nuova cultura editoriale costruita sulla gestione intelligente delle risorse.